Praise for the Innovative Leadership Workbook for Physician Leaders

If you go into a bookstore and head to the aisle marked Leadership you will be overwhelmed by the number of materials available. Where should I begin? How can I use this information to enhance my ability as a leader? The authors point out that leadership development is hard work and requires knowledge acquisition and careful introspection. The workbook is an interactive first person leadership exercise that will help you hone your leadership skills, emotional intelligence, communication and team building. Through exercises that will help you develop your personal professional vision, your story and a detailed SWOT analysis of your leadership skills you will begin your journey to transforming and unlocking your leadership potential. To enhance the learning moments you will follow a budding level 5 leader; Susan, as she completes her assessment and plan. I am pleased to highly recommend this book as a valuable adjunct to your leadership development.

E. Christopher Ellison, MD
Interim Dean, College of Medicine
CEO, Faculty Group Practice
Senior Associate Vice President for Health Sciences
Vice Dean for Clinical Affairs
The Ohio State University College of Medicine

Uncertainty in the current health care landscape requires transformational leadership that is both strategic and responsive to operational challenges and opportunities. The Innovative Leadership Workbook for Physician Leaders is a must-read for physicians who are either considering taking on new leadership roles or seasoned professionals, who wish to assess their current leadership skills and knowledge, uncovering new opportunities for professional growth. Metcalf and colleagues affirm the importance of self-awareness as the starting point for this learning opportunity, challenging the reader to consider his or her own strengths and weaknesses prior to taking on teams and transforming culture. This workbook is exactly the tool we need to remain agile as leaders and stay ahead of the changes in health care.

Eve Higginbotham SM, MD
Vice Dean, Inclusion and Diversity
Senior Fellow, Leonard Davis Institute of Health Economics
Professor of Ophthalmology Scheie Eye Institute
Perelman School of Medicine
University of Pennsylvania

The essentials of leadership development are part of the education of all those in the medical profession. In medicine and leadership it is about personal reflection, listening and learning in new ways, exploring your life goals and pursuing personal and professional growth. Resources like The Innovative Leadership Workbook for Physician Leaders bring us innovative tools that invite not only a scientific approach to leadership development, but a personal and thoughtful approach to this process. This will be a welcome addition to our work in training our current and future physician leaders.

Linda C. Stone, MD
Special Assistant to the Dean for Humanism and Professionalism
The Ohio State University College of Medicine

The field of medicine is changing rapidly and physicians and others involved in healthcare need more effective ways of being, thinking, and collaborating to deal successfully with the corresponding challenges. This workbook provides important practical tools for physicians in all fields to build the leadership skills required to navigate the future successfully!

Rustin M. Moore, DVM, PhD, Diplomate ACVS
Bud and Marilyn Jenne Professor
Associate Executive Dean
Executive Director, Veterinary Medical Center, College of Veterinary Medicine
College of Veterinary Medicine, The Ohio State University

Practical, timely and readable, this workbook is an absolute must read for every physician leader. Follow the activities, guidelines, and suggestions and you will contribute to a thriving organization, and make the impact you want to make.

Robert E. Falcone, M.D. Clinical Professor of Surgery,
The Ohio State University College of Medicine and Wexner Medical Center
Past President Grant Medical Center

In times of dramatic change in hospital systems and patient delivery models, it is critical for physician leaders to understand and align key elements of the system with their practices. This workbook emphasizes the inner work of leading oneself as well as the outer process of connecting personal values and actions to the organization's culture and systems. Physician leaders use the innovative leadership framework will position their organizations for success in serving patients and operating effectively.

Andrew Manzer, President and CEO at Schuyler Hospital

The Innovative Leadership Workbook was a valuable introspective exercise to define what I want to change about myself in order to become a better more effective leader. It helped me develop a road map to further my leadership development. It gave me more insight into myself so that I can meet the challenges of today's healthcare environment. These challenges have never been greater and navigating through them can only be enhanced through this type of exercise.

David N. Quinn, MD
Partner, Atlanta Gastroenterology Associates, LLC

INNOVATIVE LEADERSHIP WORKBOOK
FOR PHYSICIAN LEADERS

Field-Tested Processes and Worksheets for Innovating Leadership and Creating Thriving Organizations

MAUREEN METCALF, MBA
JAMES K.STOLLER, MD, MS
SHERYL PFEIL, MD
MIKE MORROW-FOX, MBA

FORWARD BY WILEY W. SOUBA, JR., MD, SCD, MBA

First Published by
Integral Publishers
1418 N. Jefferson Ave.
Tucson, AZ 85712

Published in the United States with printing and distribution in the United Kingdom, Australia, and the European Union.

ISBN: 978-0-9904419-4-6

First Printing December 2014

Cover Design, Graphics and Layout by
Creative Spot - www.creativespot.com

Acknowledgments

Contributing authors who helped to make this book a reality:
Wiley W. Souba, Jr., MD, ScD, MBA and Belinda Gore, Ph.D.

This book represents the synthesis of twenty-five years of research, work experience, and consulting for each of the primary authors. It integrates best practices from consulting firms, colleagues, nonprofits, and clients. We would first like to acknowledge our former employers for providing practical opportunities to learn and build strong skills in physician leadership, marketing, consulting, organizational change, large-scale systems change, and strategic thinking. It was this solid foundation that allowed us to create this methodology.

As a theoretical foundation, we worked with or studied the work of many thought leaders in the fields of leadership development, developmental psychology, and integral theory. The theoretical giants on whose hard work we built the Innovative Leadership and Organizational Transformation models include Terri O'Fallon, Ph.D., Susanne Cook-Greuter, Ph.D., Hilke Richmer, Ph.D., Roxanne Howe-Murphy, Ed.D., and Ken Wilber. These leaders shared not only their theories, but ongoing guidance and encouragement, helping to create a solid framework that is comprehensive and theoretically grounded.

Thanks to:

Friends and colleagues who served as constant cheerleaders and readers, made suggestions, listened to stories and dreams about the book, and helped make it come to fruition; the teachers, trainers, and mentors who taught how to lead—and when to follow.

Clients as well as graduate students who gave feedback on the book by virtue of doing graduate work using the fieldbook and writing articles that are incorporated into the foundation for this book.

Family who provided continual support and encouragement as well as inspiring us to be thoughtful, dedicated to work, and to contribute to the world in a meaningful way.

Publisher and friend, Russ Volckmann, Ph.D.

Graphic design and layout firm Creative Spot, Editorial team Mary Wood, Sara Phelps, and Eric Philippou as well as editors, reviewers, endorsers, thought partners, and countless others who spent untold hours making this possible.

Table of Contents

FOREWORD

Forward by Wiley W. Souba, Jr., MD, ScD, MBA

By any objective measure, the amount of painful, gut-wrenching change in health care continues to increase. Transformational change is always traumatic because in the process of taking it on, each of us must, in a very real sense, reinvent ourselves. We must change our assumptions, our cognitive frameworks, our ways of being and acting, and our ways of collaborating with one another. Jettisoning our familiar practices that are holding us back may make sense intellectually but rewiring the neural networks that underpin these habits can be overwhelming. It is no wonder that we don't greet change with open arms. Understandably, we avoid significant change like the plague.

Avoidance, however, is no longer an option. Intense pressure from powerful stakeholders—big business, patients, legislators, and payers—is driving the healthcare transformation imperative. This leaves us with three options. We can choose to disengage, arguing that the health care conundrum is too complex to tackle, not our problem, and certainly not our fault. In so doing, we shortchange the future of our children and most Americans. Secondly, we could decide to continue pounding away, hoping for a future that is a continuation of the past. Hope is a good thing but it is not an executable strategy.[1] Lastly, we can choose to revise the way in which we think about (make sense of) these challenges, and more specifically, revise the way in which we develop physicians who are more effective leaders going forward. Until and unless we re-language (reframe) our challenges, we will not alter, in any kind of meaningful way, our results.

How do we shift our thinking when the shackles of our long-standing cognitive maps are so entrenched and hidden? This workbook offers several assessments, tools, and practices to help you, as a leader, begin to examine your thinking and identify areas where you may need to transcend your current practices. While this process is not an easy one—it invites you to change how you see yourself in the world—it is an important part of developing yourself as a physician leader in a complex and convoluted environment.

Creating Leaders

Teaching people about leadership is different from creating leaders.[2] Teaching leadership uses a third-person approach to impart someone else's knowledge, which grants learners limited access to the being and actions of effective leaders. In contrast, creating leaders requires a first-person methodology, which provides direct access to what it means to be a leader and what it means to exercise good leadership in real time, with real results. Many health care transformation efforts run amuck because they overlook this distinction. This workbook emphasizes the inner work of leading oneself as well as the outer process of connecting personal values and actions to the organization's culture. Leaders use the innovative leadership framework to learn what it is to be a leader and what it means to exercise leadership behaviors effectively by making use of a model that distinguishes *being* a leader as the foundation for the leader's actions.

Why is the *being* of leadership foundational? Simply, because if you're not being a leader, it is impossible to act like a leader.[3] Because our understanding of what it means to *be*—a physician, a medical student, a researcher, a leader—is changing, a more effective approach to developing leaders starts with four pillars of being a leader—awareness, commitment, integrity, and authenticity—as the ontological foundation for what leaders know and do.[4] This way of understanding leadership is core to the basic tenets of professionalism. The workbook will walk you through a series of self-assessments and reflection questions to increase your level of conscious awareness. You will build a development plan and enlist a support group in helping you meet your goals thereby creating an implicit commitment to yourself and to your team. The exercises and reflection questions invite you to examine what you believe and how those beliefs impact your actions. When they are not aligned, you will identify the misalignments and have the opportunity to bring your actions into integrity with your beliefs and to act in ways that are authentic.

Accessing Leadership

When we think of the word "access," it tends to bring to mind the notion of making something available so as to utilize it, apply it, or take advantage of it (e.g., our bank account, the internet, the patient's medical record). The idea that leadership is something we access may seem odd as we generally think of leadership as an ability that people just have or don't have. However, when we recognize that leadership is about expanding our range of ways of being, thinking, and behaving so we can be more effective in dealing with those challenges for which conventional strategies are inadequate, the notion of access makes more sense.[5] Without the ability to access new ways of being and acting, we will default to what is comfortable whenever we are called to take on a major leadership challenge and our results will be mediocre at best. The innovative leadership framework in this workbook combines personality-type tools to help you understand your innate inclinations and how they impact your leadership capabilities. The framework also includes a developmental perspective that looks at how you make meaning of the world. It is this meaning-making process that matures through a series of stages that increases your capacity as a leader. The workbook is designed to help you as a leader identify your current competence and build it, thereby giving you greater access to your personal leadership capacity.

Access to leadership occurs primarily through first-person and third-person approaches, although the former tends to be disregarded. Observing leaders - and then describing, measuring, and categorizing their behaviors and traits—uses a third-person methodology. This third-person approach to studying leadership, which emphasizes what leaders know, have, and do, is theoretical and inferential but continues to be the most common leadership pedagogy.[2] Theories, explanations, and textbooks provide us with third-person access to leadership, but, in and of themselves, they do not impart what is required to be a leader, much as textbooks do not teach what it is to be a physician.

Rather than teaching leadership from a theoretical (third-person) vantage point, the first-person perspective teaches leadership as it is experienced. It is important to recognize that you and I do not lead from a theoretical standpoint; rather, we lead moment-to-moment, situation-to-situation in the way we experience leadership "as lived," that is, from a first-person point of view.[6] Such subjective experiences (first-person data) cannot be described using a third-person perspective. The distinctiveness of the first-person "as-lived/lived-through" approach lies in its capacity to disclose the hidden contexts that shape the ways of being, thinking, and acting that are the source of the leader's performance.[2] When one exercises leadership "as lived," concurrently informed by theories, one tends to be in one's "A" game. When using this workbook, you will be directly engaging in leadership development activities and reflection practices. This workbook is an attempt to integrate first-person and third-person learning. The first two chapters focus on the third-person theoretical frameworks of innovative leadership and physician leadership competencies. The book then shifts from third-person to first-person perspective as it asks you, as the leader, to complete a series of worksheets and reflection questions that explore yourself as an authentic person. You will explore your personal vision and values then develop a plan that helps you build yourself into the leader who can bring that vision into the world in a manner that is consistent with your values. The majority of the book is designed to lead you through an interactive process that helps you have the first-hand experience of yourself being a leader.

In order to gain access to more effective ways of leading, we must first expose our engrained beliefs and worldviews about leadership (e.g., I can't look incompetent, I need to be right, I must have the answers) that are limiting us. This will allow us to relax those limiting (and often veiled) ways of being and acting that have become our automatic go-to formulas (e.g., making excuses, not holding ourselves and others accountable, blaming others) that actually constrain our freedom to lead.[4] By probing this space you will explore your worldviews in general and your leadership presuppositions specifically. The authors recommend you take the MAP assessment to determine your worldview along with other assessments that help you determine your personality type and leadership behaviors. The combination of tools will give you a comprehensive view of who you are and what you do.

Mastering Language

The primary tool we use to gain access to leadership is language. In other words, discourse (with ourselves and others) is the medium through which we access and understand the world. Language allows us to bring our leadership challenges into sharper focus, allowing us to see details and "make sense" more clearly. Thus, the transformative power of language resides in its ability to create new futures. This workbook will immerse you in journaling exercises and conversations with others who are engaging in a similar process, thereby establishing a supportive network. Through the transformative power of conversation with your support team, in conjunction with the journaling exercises, you will create your own new futures through who you are becoming as leaders.

Because many of the changes that are taking place in health care are inevitable, mastering context as a leader is critical. Content (i.e., whatever we are dealing with) is always perceived through a linguistic context and, as human beings, we have the freedom to recontextualize our leadership challenges by shifting the context. Once we shift our context, “we can be a different kind of leader. When we change our thinking and speaking, a different reality becomes available to us. Shifts in our mental maps generate new possibilities for actions and outcomes not previously accessible. Only by means of language can we lead ourselves, each and every day, to become the wiser, more effective leaders that we must become.”[6] The workbook aids you in your process of recontextualizing by using a framework for reflection questions that ask you: What are your beliefs? Why do you do what you do? What do we, as an organization, value? How do we produce this value through our systems and processes? In revisiting your leadership challenges using this analytical approach, they will become more accessible and more “hittable.”[7]

Curiously, as your leadership evolves, you will likely discover that the increase in your effectiveness won’t be, first and foremost, because you acquired another technical skill—rather, it will be because the context inside of which you operate has changed.[5] A different “you” will show up. In other words, the improvement in your effectiveness will be less the result of having grasped some new theory and more a function of having altered the context through which you “perceive” your leadership challenges. This amazing capacity—to go beyond our ordinary selves to unleash our best selves—is unique to human beings and is only possible because we are not determined by a *what,* like an entity, but by a *who* that is shaped by our choices over time.[6]

References

1. Souba W. Brock Starr: a leadership fable. Journal of Surgical Research. 2009. 155: 1-6.
2. Souba W. The phenomenology of leadership. Open Journal of Leadership. In press.
3. Souba W. The science of leading yourself: A missing piece in the healthcare reform puzzle. Open Journal of Leadership 2013; 2 (3): 45–55.
4. Souba W. The being of leadership. Philosophy, Ethics, and Humanities in Medicine 2011; 6 (5). Available at http://www.ncbi.nlm.nih.gov/pmc/articles/PMC3050817/
5. Souba W. Health care transformation begins with you. Academic Medicine. In press. Available at http://www.ncbi.nlm.nih.gov/pubmed/25340365
6. Souba W. Rethinking Leadership Development. The Pharos, Summer 2014, 2-6. Available at http://alphaomegaalpha.org/pharos/PDFs/2014-3-Editorial.pdf
7. Souba W. A new model of leadership performance in health care. Acad Med 2011; 86: 1241–52

INTRODUCTION

INNOVATIVE LEADERSHIP FOR PHYSICIAN LEADERS

Leadership plays a critical role in any health care organization's long-term success, and innovation has become a strategic necessity in today's health care environment. In short, physician leadership and innovation have a greater impact today than ever before. Despite the volume of resources exploring both leadership and innovation, most approaches provide merely anecdotal directional solutions that lack sufficient information to actually allow leaders to make measureable change. Add to this equation the impact a diverse workforce and increasing competition have on health care organizations, and leaders face an even greater challenge.

As the health care landscape becomes more complicated, the need for strong leadership increases at an ever-increasing pace. Physician and hospital leaders face more complex challenges as health care reform moves forward along with increasing competition and downward price pressures. The annual survey of top issues confronting hospitals, conducted by the American College of Healthcare Executives' (ACHE's) in 2012, asked respondents to rank eleven issues affecting their hospitals in order of importance and to identify specific areas of concern within each of those issues. The survey was sent to 1,202 community hospital CEOs who are ACHE members, of whom 472, or 39 percent, responded. Financial challenges again ranked No. 1 on the list of hospital CEOs' top concerns in 2012, making it their No. 1 concern for the last nine years. Patient safety and quality ranked second. Health care reform implementation, which had been the No. 2 concern since it was introduced to the survey in 2009, moved to No. 3 in 2012. (www.ache.org/pubs/research/ceoissues.cfm)

In this continuously changing environment, the importance of strong physician leadership is accelerating at the same time that many physician leaders are retiring.

> ***One primary reason for a potential leadership void is the pending retirement of the baby boom generation. Health care organizations have only recently begun to invest in developing their leaders. A 1995 survey of 122 CEO's of healthcare institutions discovered that 31% of these organizations offered in-house leadership programs. In 2002, the health care industry spent only 1.25% of their payroll on training and development while the top corporations spent 4% of payroll on these activities***
>
> —Hopkins, O'Neil, FitzSimons, Bailin, Stoller
> *Leadership and Organization in Healthcare: Lessons from the Cleveland Clinic, 2011*

With this rapid rate of change, questions on how to lead and where to innovate remain puzzlingly philosophically: What is the role of physician leadership in a time of looming uncertainty? How will organizations innovate to overcome challenges that are largely unprecedented? In a new climate of business, is there a formula for creating success in both areas?

> ***Every system, including the human operating system, is built to get the results it gets. Moreover, every system has a design limit, which when reached cannot be surpassed unless it undergoes transformation. For human beings, reinvention means new ways of being, thinking and acting. Not surprisingly, reinvention and mastery are tightly linked.***
>
> ***All of us, regardless of our talents, must learn to lead ourselves. "Conventional thinking", writes Lee Thayer, "always and inevitably leads to conventional results" (Thayer, 2004). Slowly but surely we are learning that the process of transforming ourselves and our organizations is not just about acquiring more knowledge or changing our business strategy but also about exposing the hidden contexts that shape our ways of being and acting and limit our opportunity set for leading ourselves and others more effectively. Change resides in new ways of being, talking, and acting, which are shaped by our underlying yet hidden beliefs and assumptions (Souba, 2009). The kind of learning required to shift our worldviews is enormously challenging, but it is essential for effective leadership in health care given the enormous disequilibrium and turbulence in the environment.***
>
> —Wiley W. Souba, *The Science of Leading Yourself: A Missing Piece in the Health Care Transformation Puzzle*, 2013

Designed to help answer those questions and to help you perform the critical self-evaluation needed to identify your hidden beliefs and assumptions required to shift your world view thereby innovating your own leadership, this workbook is fundamentally about physician leadership, yet equally an account of applying innovation.

This workbook explores a number of approaches to elaborate on both areas, not just conceptually, but tangibly by providing exercises designed to enhance your leadership skills. Becoming a better physician leader and optimizing innovation jointly hinge on your ability to authentically examine your own inner makeup and diligently address some challenging limitations. Leadership innovation can be accelerated through the use of a structured process involving your own self-exploration, allowing you to authentically enhance your leadership beyond tactical execution. While we provide a process, we want to be clear that each reader will use this process in a way that is effective for him. We are all facing different challenges and relate to leadership development in different ways. Some of us are new to the practice of medicine and others will have decades of experience. Each of us will use this workbook slightly differently. With that in mind, we tried to create a framework that is actionable and easy to follow. The process of leadership growth can itself be challenging especially when it requires exploration of hidden beliefs and assumptions and changes to overall worldview—the workbook should be easy to understand and follow.

Despite their collective value, many conventional applications of leadership and innovation have often proven elusive and even problematic in real-world scenarios. For example, if the leadership team of a struggling organization drives initiatives that focus solely on making innovative changes to incentives, procedures, and services, without also advancing strategic purpose, culture, and team cohesiveness, they will ultimately miss the greater potential to create a meaningful turn-around in the organization. Productivity and system improvements are certainly critical, but how employees make sense of their work experience is equally vital to team engagement and commitment. Innovating products and improving functionality—without also creating a better team environment or a more supportive organizational culture—often appears to pay off in the short term, yet produces lopsided decision-making and shortsighted leadership that has lasting adverse consequences.

Knowing that the future of organizations is irrevocably tied to a world of erratic change, we can no longer afford to improve our systems and offerings without equally advancing our leadership capacity. Leadership empathy and the ability to inspire cultural alignment, along with other important leadership activities, will make a significant impact on your organization and must be implemented as shrewdly as strategic planning.

> ***McKinsey research and client experience suggest that half of all efforts to transform organizational performance fail either because senior managers don't act as role models for change or because people in the organization defend the status quo. In other words, despite the stated change goals, people on the ground tend to behave as they did before. Equally, the same McKinsey research indicates that if companies can identify and address pervasive mind-sets at the outset, they are four times more likely to succeed in organizational-change efforts than are companies that overlook this stage.***
>
> —Nate Boaz and Erica Ariel Fox
> *Change Leader, Change Thyself*, McKinsey Quarterly, 2014

Combining physician leadership with innovation, then, requires you to transform the way you perceive yourself, others, and your role as a physician leader.

> ***Unless one knows how to lead one's self, it would be presumptuous for anyone to be able to lead others effectively...Leading one's self implies cultivating the skills and processes to experience a higher level of self-identity beyond one's ordinary, reactive ego level...To get beyond their "ordinary, reactive ego", effective leaders relentlessly work on "un-concealing" the prevailing mental maps that they carry around in their heads. This unveiling is critical because leaders are more effective when they are not limited by their hidden frames of reference and taken-for-granted worldviews. This new way of understanding leadership requires that leaders spend more time learning about and leading themselves.***
>
> —Wiley W. Souba, *The Science of Leading Yourself: A Missing Piece in the Health Care Transformation Puzzle*

By earnestly looking at your own experience—including motivations, inclinations, interpersonal skills, proficiencies, and worldview—you can optimize your effectiveness in the current dynamic environment. Through reflection, you learn to balance the hard skills you have acquired through experience with the meaningful introspection attained through deep examination—all the while setting the stage for further growth. In essence, you discover how to strategically and tactically innovate leadership the same way you innovate in other aspects of your profession.

Marrying Physician Innovation and Leadership

Leadership needs innovation in the same way innovation demands leadership, and by marrying the two, you can better your capacity for growth and improved effectiveness. Let's explore innovating leadership in a more tangible way by defining it in practical terms.

What Does Innovating Leadership Really Mean?

Let's start with the definition of leadership as a uniquely human activity that is intended to move an organization forward such that it improves the lives of the people it serves and simultaneously takes into consideration the rightful interests of the organizational members.

It is important to note that each individual leader will perform the activity of leadership in a manner that is authentic to his or her unique skills, abilities, personality, beliefs, values, and other influencing factors such as brain chemistry. This book references several models to help you build a general understanding and create a common language to discuss how we develop as leaders. We want to point out that effective leadership encompasses both the science of leading and the heart of the leader. Effective leadership requires heartfelt care, compassion, and authenticity to be truly effective. This does not mean leaders are soft, but rather they demonstrate compassion when taking tough action. Being a good scientist and understanding the theory is a good start but insufficient if the leader does not demonstrate deep care for the people being led and the people being served. This care is addressed when we talk about the competency of emotional intelligence and is a thread through the entire workbook.

> ***Most approaches to leadership development are based on the assumption that inculcating people with specific characteristics and traits will make them effective leaders. However, effective leaders know that leadership does not come from imitating certain styles or memorizing an article on the attributes of successful leaders. Barker (1997) reminds us that 'we have become mired in an obsession with the rich and powerful, with traits, characteristics, behaviors, roles, styles, and abilities of people who by hook or by crook have obtained high positions, [yet] we know little if anything more about leadership.' Leading oneself is less about styles and traits and more about discovering one's natural self-expression. This is a key prerequisite for leading others.***
>
> —Wiley W. Souba, *The Science of Leading Yourself: A Missing Piece in the Health Care Transformation Puzzle*

Although useful, such approaches are still, essentially, formulas for imitating leadership, and are likely ineffectual over the long term. Innovating leadership cannot be applied as a monolithic theory, or as a simple prescriptive measure. It occurs through your own intellect and stems from your own unique sensibilities.

In order to enhance this unique awareness process, you will need a greater foundational basis from which to explore both innovation and leadership, which means talking about them in an entirely different context.

Physician leadership **is a process of influencing people strategically and tactically, effecting change in intentions, actions, culture, and systems to move the healthcare organization forward such that it improves the lives of the people it serves and simultaneously takes into consideration the rightful interests of the organizational members.**

Leadership influences individual intentions and organizational cultural norms by inspiring purpose and creating alignment. It equally influences an individual's actions and an organization's efficiencies through tactical decisions.

Innovation, as an extension of leadership, refers to the novel ways in which we advance that influence throughout the organization.

Innovation is a novel advancement that shapes organizations personally, behaviorally, culturally, and systematically.

In our experience, leadership and innovation are innately connected and share a deep commonality. In addition to linking the relationship of leadership to innovation, notice that we're also revealing it as an essential part of our individual experience. Just as with leadership and innovation, the way you uniquely experience and influence the world is defined through a mutual interplay of personal, behavioral, cultural, and systematic events. These same core dimensions that ground leadership and innovation also provide a context and mirror for your total experience in any given moment or on any given occasion. Optimally, then, leadership is influencing through an explicit balancing of those core dimensions. Innovation naturally follows as a creative advancement of this basic alignment.

Therefore, marrying leadership with innovation allows you to ground and articulate both in a way that creates a context for dynamic personal development—and, dynamic personal development is required to lead innovative transformative change

Innovating physician leadership means leaders influence by equally engaging their personal intention and action with the organization's culture and systems to move the healthcare organization forward such that it improves the lives of the people it serves and simultaneously takes into consideration the rightful interests of the organizational members.

Though we are defining innovative physician leadership very broadly, we are also making a distinct point: *The core aspects that comprise your experience—whether it is Leader* ***intention*** *or* ***action,*** *organizational* ***culture,*** *or* ***systems****—are inextricably interconnected. If you affect one, you affect them all.*

Innovative physician leadership is based on the recognition that these four dimensions exist simultaneously in all experiences, and already influence every interactive experience we have. So if, for example, you implement a strategy to realign an organization's value system over the next five years, you will also affect personal motivations (intentions), behavioral outcomes, and organizational culture. Influencing one aspect—in this case, functional systems—affects the other aspects, since all four dimensions mutually shape each other. To deny the mutual interplay of any one of the four dimensions misses the full picture. You can only innovate your leadership by comprehensively addressing all aspects. In sum, leadership innovation is the process of improving leadership that allows already successful leaders to raise the bar on their performance and the performance of their organizations.

An innovative leader is defined as someone who consistently delivers results using:

- Strategic leadership that inspires individual intentions and goals and organizational vision and culture
- Tactical leadership that influences an individual's actions and the organization's systems and processes
- Holistic leadership that aligns all core dimensions: individual intention and action, along with organizational culture and systems

The Opportunity of Innovative Leadership

Although the overwhelming focus of today's health care organizational changes is on system functionality, it is only part of the total picture. Being guided by more strategically inclusive decisions may be the difference between managing dysfunction and creating tangible success. Your leadership must consider a more balanced definition of innovation that comprehensively aligns vision, teams, and systems, and integrates enhanced leadership perspective with system efficiency.

This balanced approach to leadership and innovation is transformative for both you and your organization, and can help you to respond more effectively to challenges within and outside the enterprise. Innovating your leadership gives you the means to successfully adapt in ways that allows optimal performance, even within the continual change and complexity of an organization. Conceptually, it synthesizes models from developmental, communications, and systems theory, delivering better insight than singular approaches. Innovative physician leadership gives you the capacity to openly recognize and critically examine aspects of yourself, as well as your organization's culture and systems, in the midst of any circumstance.

Defining What an Innovative Physician Leader Does

What are specific behaviors that differentiate an innovative leader from a traditional leader? A successful innovative leader is one who can continually:

- Clarify and effectively articulate vision, and link that vision to attainable strategic initiatives
- Develop oneself and influence the development of others
- Build effective teams by helping colleagues engage their own leadership strengths
- Cultivate alliances and partnerships
- Anticipate and aggressively respond to both challenges and opportunities
- Develop robust and resilient solutions
- Develop and test hypotheses like a scientist
- Measure, learn, and refine on an ongoing basis

To further illustrate some of the qualities of innovative leadership, we offer this comparison between traditional leadership and innovative leadership:

TRADITIONAL LEADERSHIP	INNOVATIVE LEADERSHIP
Leader is guided primarily by desire for personal success, and peripherally by organizational success.	Leader is humbly guided by a more altruistic vision of success based on both performance and the value of the organization's positive impact.
Leader decides in a "command and control" style; leader has all the answers.	Leader leverages team for answers as part of the decision-making process.
Leader picks a direction in "black/white" manner; tends to dogmatically stay the course.	Leader perceives and behaves like a scientist: continually experimenting, measuring, and testing for improvement and exploring new models and approaches.

TRADITIONAL LEADERSHIP	INNOVATIVE LEADERSHIP
Leader focuses on being technically correct and in charge.	Leader is continually learning and developing self and others.
Leader manages people to perform by being autocratic and controlling.	Leader motivates people to perform through strategic focus, mentoring and coaching, and interpersonal intelligence.
Leader tends to the numbers and primarily utilizes quantitative measures that drive those numbers.	Leader tends to financial performance, customer satisfaction, employee engagement, community impact, and cultural cohesion.

Getting the Most from the Workbook

Increasingly, it is becoming apparent that leaders must learn how to access leadership in the first person rather than mentally reaching for the latest best seller or a 5-step algorithm. In other words, when someone explains leadership to you, their account gives you no direct access to leadership. You may be able to recite many leadership books, but until you experience for yourself first-hand what it is to deal with a complex leadership challenge and to confront your fears and inadequacies in dealing with it, you cannot be a leader or exercise leadership effectively. It is for just this reason that we wrote a work book that provides you the opportunity to have those first-hand experiences throughout the book.

As your first opportunity to experience leadership development first-hand, take a moment to think about why you purchased this workbook. Setting goals and understanding your intentions and expectations about the exercises will help you identify and drive your desired results.

In order to help clarify, consider the following questions:

- What are the five to seven events and choices that brought you to where you are professionally and personally?
- What stands out in the list you have made? Are there any surprises or patterns?
- How did these events and choices contribute to choosing to buy and use this workbook?
- What do you hope to gain from your time investment in leadership development?
- What meaningful impact will it have professionally and personally?

In addition to reflecting on the questions, we recommend you use the learning practices to help you get the most out of this investment in your development. It is our experience that people who adhere to the following practices tend to have a deeper and more enriching overall experience, and more effectively take advantage of what this workbook has to offer.

What are "Learning Practices"?

Now that you have this workbook in hand, you may be wondering, "What can I actually do to get better as a physician leader?" It's one thing to know that you need to "think more strategically," or improve at "giving performance feedback and coaching." It's something completely different to translate that into practical actions that bring about lasting change, growth, and development.

Since most of us spend over ninety percent of our work time working rather than in training programs or workshops, time on the job and our day-to-day experience are our best and most accessible opportunity to learn. We just need to know how to use our experience to grow and develop.

Learning Practices are actions you can take to accelerate and enhance experiential learning and determine whether you proactively pursue learning in your day-to-day work life, or focus only on getting the job done. Leaders who consistently and rigorously use the Learning Practices learn significantly more and faster while achieving better results. The following key learning practices have significant potential for growing and accelerating your ability to learn from experience:

LEARNING PRACTICES		RELATED ACTION OR BEHAVIOR
Take responsibility for your own learning and development.	→	Be 100% responsible for the outcome of your engagement with this material.
Approach new assignments/ opportunities with openness to experience and positive intention to learn.	→	Each assignment will provide you with opportunities to learn things you did not know about yourself or others; take advantage of these opportunities even if you think you might already know the answers.
Seek and use feedback.	→	Identify who will provide you with feedback and use what you learn about yourself to learn and grow (see chapter on building your team).
Develop a clear understanding of your strengths and areas for development.	→	Determine which assessments will give you the most valuable set of feedback (see chapter on analyzing your strengths and situation).
Ask great questions and demonstrate curiosity.	→	Remain openly curious through the process; ongoing learning is an important key to success in leadership development.
Listen in a manner that leaves you open to personal transformation.	→	Listen intently, deeply, and empathically, identifying ways to not only change your behavior, but also how you see the world.
Respond to experience with adaptability and flexibility.	→	Your ability to respond to unexpected situations with finesse will position you well during your development process (see resilience element in Innovative Leadership).
Actively reflect and practice mindfulness.	→	Take the time to answer the refection questions and be fully present while you are doing the exercises.

LEARNING PRACTICES		RELATED ACTION OR BEHAVIOR
Actively experiment with new approaches to learning.	→	Find opportunities where you can safely apply new ways of learning skills or behaviors such as special projects or volunteer roles.
Closely observe and learn from others.	→	Find a mentor or person you believe has mastered the skills you are trying to develop and closely observe what this person does and how they do it. Try to "steal" or adopt the techniques they use to succeed.
Participate as fully as possible.	→	Complete all the exercises to the best of your abilities. Apply the concepts and skills that work best for you, and modify those that do not.
Practice good life management.	→	Invest time at scheduled intervals to work on the materials when you are mentally and emotionally at your best.
Lean into optimal discomfort; take risks without overwhelming yourself.	→	Be candid, open, and direct. Allow yourself to be curious and vulnerable.
Take the process seriously, and more importantly take yourself lightly. Make this a positive and rewarding experience.	→	Allow yourself balance. Find the lesson and humor in both your successes and mistakes. Most importantly, have fun!

To develop the learning mindset, use these guidelines:

1. Turn the switch to "on." Decide that you want to develop the learning mindset and commit to making it an area of your ongoing growth and development.

2. Be intentional about learning. Use "preflection," orienting yourself toward learning every day by thinking about and envisioning, in advance, what you want to learn. Use reflection by replaying the day's events in your mind and thinking about what you learned.

3. Use mantras to reprogram your autopilot. All of us operate on autopilot most of the time. This is both a good thing and a bad thing. While it helps to automate repetitive tasks and actions so we don't have to think about them, it also leads us to stop paying attention to important information in the world around us. On autopilot, we work on the basis of old assumptions, beliefs, and data. If you want to start learning more from experience, find your own personal mantra to orient your mind toward learning. Here are a few examples:

   - "Development is about getting better and better, not being perfect."
   - "Never give up."
   - "It's not whether I win or lose. I win if I learn, grow, and develop."
   - "Observe. Learn. Improve. Get better."

4. Make it conscious until it is automatic. If it doesn't seem natural to you to go through your day with an eye toward learning, one way to counter that is to repeatedly and consciously do things that someone with a strong Learning Mindset would do. For example, purposely seek out new experiences that take you out of your comfort zone, and when engaging in those experiences make it your goal to learn as much as you can through the experience. Over time, you will begin to develop new neural pathways that contribute to new habits of mind and behavior: The Learning Mindset.

To begin using learning practices as tools to accelerate and enhance your progress from experiential learning, start with taking responsibility for your own growth and development. Until you actually ***own*** your development—***taking, not just accepting, responsibility*** for your own learning and growth—you are a passive bystander who is waiting or sleep-walking through life. Unless you take responsibility for your own growth and development, learning may or may not happen, and, if it does, it will be accidental, incidental, serendipitous, and tacit. And you will be missing out on the biggest developmental arena available to leaders: day-to-day work experience.

As you face the challenges of physician leaders, remember that the most effective leaders have the ability to transform their experiences into growth and development. And the greater the challenge, the more significant is the opportunity to develop as a leader. If you have a Learning Mindset and consistently and rigorously put the learning practices into action, you will learn significantly more, faster, and as a result you'll perform at a higher level and create greater value for your company and for yourself.

Adopting the Learning Mindset, and using Learning Practices is not as simple as it may seem, and as Benjamin Franklin put it in his *New Farmer's Almanac*, "There are three things extremely hard: steel, a diamond, and to know one's self." On the surface, the logic is clear: attitudes lead to behaviors. And, you may already be thinking, "Of course, I have a Learning Mindset! I do some of those Learning Practices all the time!" Unfortunately, most of us do a pretty poor job of assessing our own competencies and capabilities. We tend to exaggerate our strengths and downplay our weaknesses. We all need to use a heightened level of self-examination and conduct an honest appraisal of ourselves as we work on developing ourselves as leaders.

How to Use the Workbook

Each chapter of the workbook builds on a series of exercises and reflection questions designed to guide you through the process of developing your own abilities as an innovative leader. We recommend that you use the following sequence to efficiently process the material:

1. ***Read Intently***

   Read through the chapter completely, as we introduce and illustrate an integrated set of concepts for each element in building innovative leadership.

2. ***Contemplate***

   Using a set of carefully chosen applications and specifically designed exercises will help to bring the concepts to life. Through a process of dynamic examination and reflection, you will be encouraged to contemplate some significant, real-life implications of change. Many of the exercises can be done on your own; others are designed to be conducted with input from your colleagues.

3. ***Link Together Your Experience***

   As you sequentially build your understanding, you will begin noticing habits and conditioned patterns that present you with clear opportunities for growth. Though you may encounter personal resistance along the way, you will also discover new and exciting strengths. As you become more adept at using these ideas, you will find yourself increasingly capable of proactive engagement with the concepts, and increasingly able to respond to situations requiring innovative leadership with greater capacity.

Once you have completed the process, you will have created a plan to grow as an innovative physician leader.

ASSESSMENT

Innovative Leadership for Physician Leaders

The following is a short self-assessment to help you identify your own scores relating to innovative leadership for physician leaders. It is organized by the five domains of Innovative Leadership. This will give you a general sense of where you want to focus your efforts. We encourage you to take this survey as a way to get a snapshot of where you excel and where you may want to focus your energies. Think about the last year when determining your answer. If you are not sure, select "Sometimes," as the survey will not score properly unless you answer each question. The survey should take about 10 minutes to complete.

Assessment Instructions:

- Complete all questions per page. Each of the five sections will appear on separate pages.
- Complete each page and calculate your score on each of the five elements of Innovative Leadership.

Score Yourself on Awareness of Leader Type

Think about how you responded to work situations over the past year and answer the following questions using this scale:

Never (1) *Rarely (2)* *Sometimes (3)* *Often (4)* *Almost always (5)*

1. I have taken a leadership type assessment such as the Enneagram, Myers-Briggs Type Indicator or DiSC, and used this information about myself to increase my effectiveness. **1 2 3 4 5**
2. I use the insight from this assessment to understand my type. Specifically, I know and understand my gifts and limitations, and try to leverage my strengths and manage my limitations. **1 2 3 4 5**
3. I have a reflection practice where I understand, actively monitor, and work with my "fixations" (negative thought patterns). **1 2 3 4 5**
4. I have a clear sense of who I am and what I contribute to the world. **1 2 3 4 5**
5. I manage my emotional reactions to allow me to respond with socially appropriate behavior. **1 2 3 4 5**
6. I am aware of what causes me stress and actively manage it. **1 2 3 4 5**
7. I have positive coping strategies. **1 2 3 4 5**
8. I actively seek ways to feel empowered even when the organization may not empower me. **1 2 3 4 5**

Total Score

- If your overall score in this category is 24 or less, it's time to pay attention to your leadership type and self-management.
- If your overall score in this category is 25 to 31, you are in the healthy range, but could still benefit from some focus on your leadership type and self-management.
- If your overall score is 32 or above, congratulations! You are self-aware and using your leadership type to increase your effectiveness.

Score Yourself on Developmental Perspective

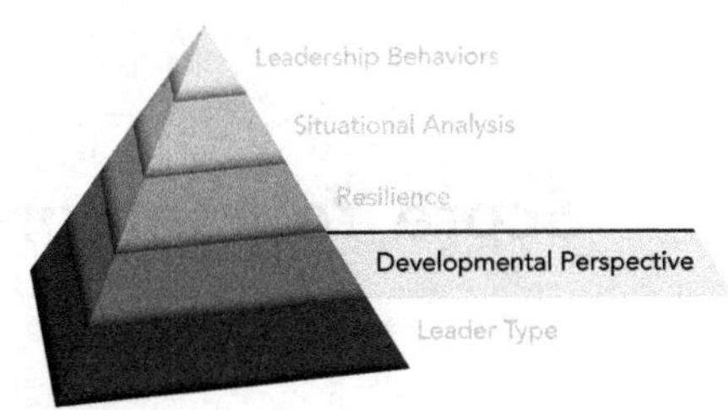

Think about how you responded to work situations over the past year and answer the following questions using this scale:

Never (1) *Rarely (2)* *Sometimes (3)* *Often (4)* *Almost always (5)*

1. I have a sense of life purpose and do work that is generally aligned with that purpose. **1 2 3 4 5**
2. I am motivated by the impact I make on the world more than on gaining personal notoriety. **1 2 3 4 5**
3. I try to live my life according to my personal values. **1 2 3 4 5**
4. I believe that collaboration across groups and organizations and cultures is important to accomplish our goals. **1 2 3 4 5**
5. I believe that getting business results must be balanced with treating people fairly and kindly. **1 2 3 4 5**
6. I consistently seek input from others to test my thinking and expand my perspective. **1 2 3 4 5**
7. I think about the impact of my work on our community and the world. **1 2 3 4 5**
8. I am open and curious, always trying new things and learning from all of them. **1 2 3 4 5**
9. I appreciate the value of rules and am willing to question them in a professional manner. **1 2 3 4 5**

Total Score

- If your overall score in this category is 27 or less, it's time to pay attention to your developmental level, including testing your current level and focusing on developing in the area of developmental perspectives.
- If your overall score in this category is 28 to 35, you are in the healthy range, but could still benefit from some focus on developing in the area of developmental perspectives.
- If your score is 36 or above, congratulations! Your developmental level appears to be aligned with innovative leadership, yet this assessment is only a subset of a full assessment.

Score Yourself on Resilience

With regard to work situations, think about your level of response over the past year and answer the following questions using this scale:

Never (1) *Rarely (2)* *Sometimes (3)* *Often (4)* *Almost always (5)*

1. I consistently take care of my physical needs such as getting enough sleep and exercise. **1 2 3 4 5**
2. I have a sense of purpose and get to do activities that contribute to that purpose daily. **1 2 3 4 5**
3. I have a high degree of self-awareness and actively manage my thoughts. **1 2 3 4 5**
4. I have a strong support system consisting of a healthy mix of friends, colleagues, and family. **1 2 3 4 5**
5. I can reframe challenges to find something of value in most situations. **1 2 3 4 5**
6. I build strong trusting relationships at work with a broad range of people. **1 2 3 4 5**
7. I am aware of my own "self-talk" and actively manage it. **1 2 3 4 5**
8. I have a professional development plan that includes gaining skills and additional perspectives from a broad range of people who think and act differently than I do. **1 2 3 4 5**

Total Score

- If your overall score in this category is 24 or less, it's time to pay attention to your resilience.
- If your overall score in this category is 25 to 31, you are in the healthy range, but could still benefit from some focus on resilience.
- If your score is 32 or above, congratulations! Although this assessment is only a subset of the full resilience assessment, you are likely performing well in the area of resilience.

Score Yourself on Situational Analysis

Think about how you responded to work situations over the past year and answer the following questions using this scale:

Never (1) *Rarely* (2) *Sometimes* (3) *Often* (4) *Almost always* (5)

1. I am aware of my own passions and values. **1 2 3 4 5**
2. My behavior consistently reflects my goals and values. **1 2 3 4 5**
3. I feel safe pushing back when I am asked to do things that are not aligned with my values. **1 2 3 4 5**
4. I am aware that my behavior and decisions as a leader have an impact on the people I work with (even if I am not directly managing them/others). **1 2 3 4 5**
5. I am deliberate about aligning my behaviors with what the organization requires and I pay attention to delivering the desired results (both results and behaviors). **1 2 3 4 5**
6. I am aware of how my values align with those of the organization and where they are misaligned; if there are misalignments, I try to find constructive ways to address these differences. **1 2 3 4 5**

Total Score

- If your overall score in this category is 18 or less, it's time to pay attention to your alignment with the organization and also the alignment of culture and systems within the organization that you are able to impact.
- If your overall score in this category is 19 to 23, you are in the healthy range, but could still benefit from some focus on alignment.
- If your score is 24 or above, congratulations! You are well aligned with the organization, and the organization's culture and systems are well-aligned.

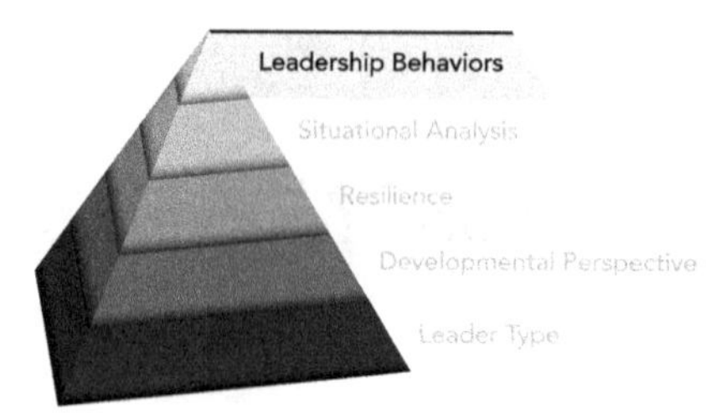

Score Yourself on Leadership Behaviors

Think about how you responded to work situations over the past year and answer the following questions using this scale:

Never (1) *Rarely (2)* *Sometimes (3)* *Often (4)* *Almost always (5)*

1. I consistently make decisions that put the best interest of the organization ahead of my personal career advancement. **1 2 3 4 5**
2. I consistently demonstrate the ability to make the tough decisions and stay the course when I know what I am doing is the right thing to do. I make these calls even when they are really tough. **1 2 3 4 5**
3. I understand the interconnections between the many elements of my hospital/practice and I am able to balance the competing commitments to make decisions that are in the best interest of the overall organization. **1 2 3 4 5**
4. I continue to learn and grow in areas outside of my comfort zone. **1 2 3 4 5**
5. I consistently seek feedback and accept it graciously even when it is less than favorable. **1 2 3 4 5**
6. I take time to mentor others, even when I am busy and provide feedback in a way that supports their ongoing growth and success. **1 2 3 4 5**
7. I know who to ask and I seek feedback from others who have differing points of view so I can synthesize their views to create comprehensive approaches and solutions. **1 2 3 4 5**

Total Score

- If your overall score in this category is 21 or less, it's time to pay attention to your leadership mindset and behaviors.
- If your overall score in this category is 22 to 28, you are in the healthy range, but could still benefit from some focus on leadership mindset and behaviors.
- If your score is 39 or above, congratulations! You have a well-developed leadership mindset and associated behaviors.

CHAPTER 1
Elements of Innovative Leadership

Too often, leaders of organizational change see the organization as an object separate of themselves...To be an effective leader, one must understand the nature of leadership, one's self, and [the] organization within the unfolding of one's day-to-day experience...[It is] clear how important it is for a leader to be the organizational change he or she seeks.

—Wiley W. Souba, *The Science of Leading Yourself: A Missing Piece in the Health Care Transformation Puzzle, 2013*

The Innovative Leadership model is designed to help you as physician leaders understand yourselves, the organizational culture and systems, and identify the changes necessary to lead a changing organization. You will use this model as the foundation for your own personal leadership development roadmap. The five elements that comprise Innovative leadership—Leader Type, Developmental Perspective, Resilience, Situational Analysis, and Leadership Behaviors—are discussed and applied throughout the balance of the book. For each of the five elements, we discuss the concept and various assessment instruments that can be used to assess your leadership within each element. In this chapter, we define and describe each element of Innovative Leadership and how they interact, and then provide a general framework for innovating how you lead. Later in chapter five you will focus in greater depth on the process to develop your leadership, leveraging each of the elements, and providing opportunities to use the instruments.

As mentioned in the forward, we use models to create a shared language for talking about and developing physician leadership. Each individual physician will use this material differently to accomplish their goals of moving your organization forward such that it improves the lives of the people it serves and simultaneously takes into consideration the rightful interests of the organizational members. This framework requires equal parts of the science of leadership and the heart of the physician who is leading. The topic of heart is addressed by competencies and behaviors that point to leading with heart such as emotional intelligence.

Figure1.1 Five Elements of Innovative Leadership

Theorists have looked at each of these elements separately, over many years, and have suggested that mastering one or two of them is typically sufficient for effective leaders. We believe that while that may have been true in a less complex world, it is no longer the case. What is unique in this approach to leadership is the overall comprehensiveness of the model. As the twenty-first century unfolds, the most effective leaders will need a much more holistic view than at any other time in history. In short, leadership excellence is a journey and while the great leader may not have mastered all five elements in this model, she will be working toward mastery of all of them.

Leader Personality Type (or Leader Type)

In this workbook, we will be talking about ***Leader Personality Type*** as the first of the five core elements (Figure 1.1) in developing Innovative Leadership. Part of the challenge in innovating leadership is learning to become more self-reflective and to put that self-reflective knowledge into practice. Looking inside yourself and examining the makeup of your inner being enables you to function in a highly grounded way, rather than operating only from the innate biases that lead to uninformed, reflexive or unconscious decision-making.

The Leader Personality Type reflects your core predispositions and attitudes as a person. Not surprisingly, these attributes critically influence who you are as a leader and how people will experience your leadership. This, as with the ancient Greek adage—"Know thyself"—is important because it will provide insight into your "default" presence and will also offer you the opportunity to use other leadership traits in appropriate ways within a situation. One way to observe this is by examining aspects of your inner being that reflect your personality. The Leader Personality Type (referred to going forward as Leader Type) is an essential foundation of your personal makeup and greatly shapes your leadership effectiveness. There are several useful tools for helping to describe leadership and personality types. Some of these tools are used by a wide range of organizations, e.g., the Myers Briggs Type Indicator (MBTI), DiSC, Big Five Personality Test, and the Enneagram. Each of these tools (or models) has particular strengths in their presentations, as well as certain weaknesses. Their overall purpose is to help you make objective sense of your thought and behavior patterns—i.e., your Leader Type—and those of other people.

> ***Self-awareness, the practice of engaging in self-reflection and achieving clarity of insight, being conscious of one's own identity, and the extent to which perceptions about one's self are accurate and compatible with others' observations, play a pivotal role in leadership. Self-aware leaders self-regulate cognitions, emotions, and behavior more effectively depending on the situation, evaluate their impact on others, and possess higher levels of emotional intelligence.***
>
> ***Thus, they become more versatile in their leadership and may perform better. Consequently, successful leader development is foremost personal development. The Enneagram, one of the most comprehensive systems for understanding personality [leader type] and human development, offers considerable merit to support leaders to become more aware of themselves and others.***
>
> —Hilke Richmer, Ed.D. An Analysis of the Effects of Enneagram-Based Leader Development on Self-Awareness: A Case Study at a Midwest Utility Company
> Doctoral Dissertation, Spalding University, 2011

As we observed through Hilke Richmer's research project, the Enneagram is one such typing model. We find the Enneagram especially powerful and we discuss it further below and in greater detail in chapter three of this book, when we review Leader Type assessments.

Your ability to use deep self-reflection relies on your development of a capacity for self-understanding and self-awareness, both features of emotional intelligence (as we will discuss further in chapter two). Both self-understanding and self-awareness allow you to expand your perspective as well as to develop a greater understanding of others. These traits associated with Leader Type support a leader's abilities to manage self, to communicate effectively with others, and to encourage personal learning. It is important to keep in mind that these personality and leadership types are generally traits that are native to your being and generally do not change significantly over the course of your life. This is an essential point: ***By understanding your type, as well as those of others around you, you can begin to see situations without the bias of your own perceptions.*** You can develop a clearer understanding, and can thus make more informed decisions with less reflexive behavior. You can learn to deeply understand the inner movements of your strengths, weaknesses, and core patterns. Leadership typing tools like the Enneagram are helpful in promoting this kind of self-knowledge and pattern recognition.

Given that we all have "blind spots" (namely, things about ourselves that we do not see but that others recognize about us), another important way to gain insight about yourself is to seek feedback from trusted colleagues, family members, and/or friends. Getting feedback in a safe way can help you understand your "real self." This is especially true because the way you appear to others can be difficult to appreciate without such feedback or the use of leadership type assessment instruments.

> ***By learning about these patterns, you can gain perspective on your life and start connecting the dots among your different experiences. Most of us have a concept about how we behave, but that idea is likely clouded and not entirely true. One of the hardest things for most people is to see themselves accurately. How astonishing it is to see through the clouds and recognize yourself clearly.***
>
> —Roxanne Howe Murphy
> *Deep Living, 2103*

Learning at this deeper level from your own inner dynamics can offer remarkable insight about areas of life that, in your own personal experience, you may either exaggerate or underemphasize.

Developmental Perspective

In this workbook, we will be talking about ***Developmental Levels and Perspectives*** as the second of the five core elements (Figure 1.1) in developing Innovative Leadership. Developmental Perspectives significantly influence how you see your role and function in the workplace, how you interact with other people, and how you solve problems. The term *Developmental Perspective* can be described as "making meaning," or how you make meaning or sense of experiences. This is important because the algorithm you use to make sense of the world influences your thoughts and actions. Incorporating these perspectives as part of your inner exploration is critical to developing Innovative Leadership.

We measure Leader Type using the Enneagram, and we measure Developmental Perspective using an assessment called the Maturity Assessment Profile [MAP]. It evaluates three primary dimensions: cognitive complexity, emotional competence, and behavior. The MAP is also a sophisticated instrument for identifying and measuring later stage, developmentally advanced leadership. This assessment is referenced in greater detail in chapter three where you determine which assessments you would like to take to support your development.

Figure 1.2 Enneagram & Developmental Perspectives

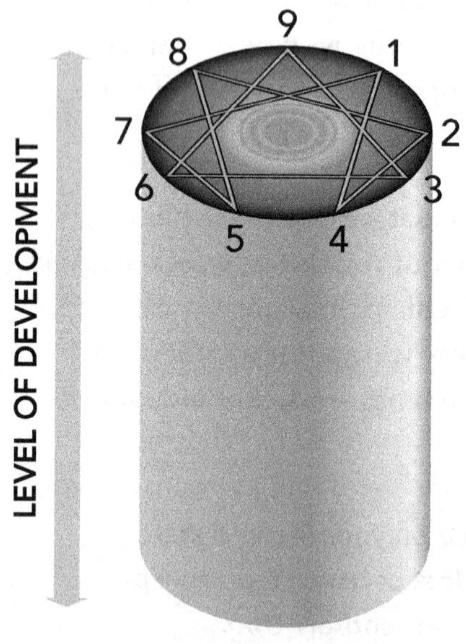

In order to connect Developmental Perspective with Leader Type, let's look at how these two core elements and models come together. While Leader Type is generally constant over your life, you have the capacity to grow and develop your leadership (developmental) perspective. In fact, leadership research strongly suggests that although your inherent Leader Type determines your tendency to lead, good leaders also develop over time. Therefore, it is often the case that leaders are both born and made. How leaders are made is best described using an approach that considers their Developmental Perspective. Type remains consistent during your life while Developmental Perspective evolves. This is an important differentiator in leadership effectiveness and allows you to see what can be changed and what should be accepted as an innate personality type.

We can also apply this model at the organizational level to help select and train leaders more effectively. Here are some additional benefits of using a model of Developmental Perspective:

- It guides leaders in determining their personal development goals and action plans using their Developmental Perspective as an important criterion.
- It is important to consider when determining which individuals and team member's best fit specific roles.
- It helps identify high-potential leaders to groom for growth opportunities.
- It helps in the hiring process to determine individual fit for a specific job.
- It helps change agents understand the perspective of others and craft solutions that meet the needs of all stakeholders.

Figure.1.3 Maslow's Hierarchy of Needs

The Developmental Perspective approach is based on research and the observation that, over time, people tend to grow and progress through a number of very distinct stages of awareness and ability. One of the best-known and tested developmental models is Abraham Maslow's hierarchy of needs, a pyramid-shaped visual aid he created to help explain his theory of psychological and physical human needs. As you ascend the steps of the pyramid, you can eventually reach a level of self-actualization.

Developmental growth occurs much like other capabilities grow in your life. Building on your Leader Type, you continue to grow, increasing access to or capacity for additional skills. We call this "transcend and include" in that you transcend the prior level/perspective and still maintain the ability to function at that perspective. Using the example of learning how to run to illustrate the process of development, you must first learn to stand and walk before you can run. And yet, as you eventually master running, you still effortlessly retain the earlier, foundational skill that allowed you to stand and walk. In other words, you can develop your capacity to build beyond the basic skills you have now by moving through more progressive stages. It is also important to note that while individuals develop the ability to run, there are many times that walking is a much more appropriate choice of movement. The successful leader has a broad repertoire of behaviors and is able to select the most appropriate one depending on the situation. This concept has been called "situational leadership."

People develop through stages at vastly differing rates, often influenced by significant events or "disorienting dilemmas." Those events or dilemmas provide opportunities to begin experiencing your world from a completely different point-of-view. The nature of those influential events can vary greatly, ranging from positive social milestones like marriage, a new job, or the birth of a child, to negative experiences, such as job loss, an accident, or the death of a loved one. These situations often trigger more lasting changes in your way of thinking and feeling altogether. Some new Developmental Perspectives can develop very gradually over time or, in some cases, emerge quite abruptly.

Some developmentally advanced people may be relatively young, while others may experience very little developmental growth over the course of their life. Adding to the complexity of developmental growth is the fact that the unfolding of Developmental Perspectives is not predictably based on age, gender, nationality, or affluence. We can sense indicators that help us identify Developmental Perspective when we listen and exchange ideas with others, engage in self-reflection, and display openness to learning. In fact, most people naturally intuit and discern what motivates others as well as what causes some of their own greatest challenges.

We believe a solid understanding of Developmental Perspectives is critical to innovating leadership and encourage you to delve into this concept in greater detail. The purpose of this workbook is to introduce you to these concepts.

Resilience

Resilience is the third key leadership concept (Figure 1.1) and can be understood in two distinct ways. First, using an engineering analogy, Resilience is viewed as how much disturbance your systems can absorb before they break down. This view highlights the sturdiness of individual systems. Second, from a leadership perspective, Resilience can be viewed as the ability to adapt in the face of erratic change while continuing to be both fluid in approach and driven toward attaining strategic goals. The first definition reflects stability and the second refers to fluidity and endurance. Addressing all aspects of Resilience is critical to optimizing it.

Among the elements essential to leadership, Resilience is unique in that it integrates the physical and psychological aspects of leader type and Developmental Perspective to create the foundation of a leader's inner stability. This foundation enables you to demonstrate fluidity and endurance as you adapt to ongoing change.

Figure1.4 Elements of Resilience

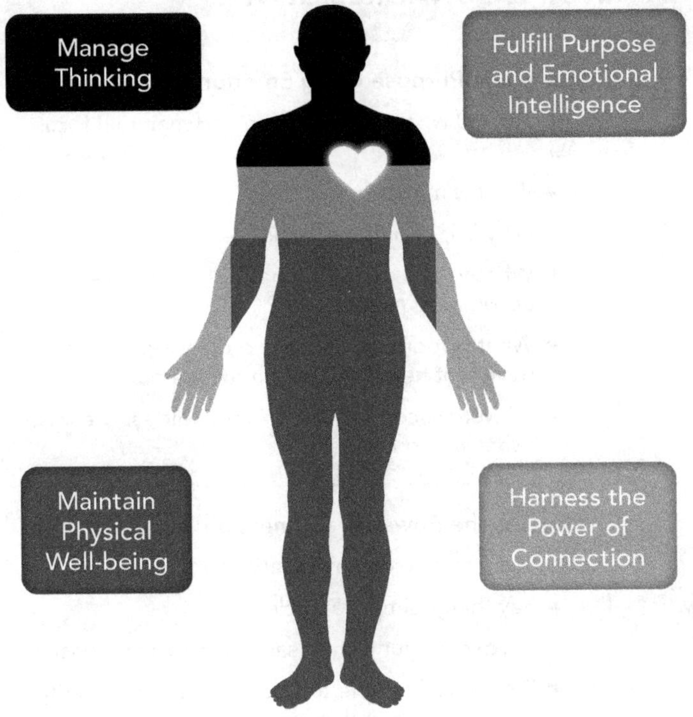

The underlying premise of Resilience is that as a leader, you need to be physically and emotionally healthy to do a good job. In addition to physical and emotional health, the resilient leader also has a clear sense of life purpose, strong emotional intelligence, and strong supportive relationships. For most people, enhancing Resilience requires a personal change.

Our model of Resilience has four categories: maintaining physical well-being, managing thinking fulfilling purpose using emotional intelligence, and harnessing the power of connection. These categories are interlinked, and all of them must be in balance to create long-term Resilience.

Leaders we work with often initially say they are too busy to take care of themselves. Finding the balance between self-care and meeting all of our daily commitments is tough. Yet, leaders are their own most important instruments of leadership, so caring for oneself is crucial. Most people fall short of their goals and over the longer term make choices for Resilience and personal health or against it. Our message here is that creating and maintaining Resilience is essential to your success. As you improve your Resilience, you will think more clearly and have a greater positive impact in your interactions with others. Investing in your Resilience supports the entire organization's effectiveness.

The following table provides questions for each of the four Resilience categories to identify opportunities for improvement.

TABLE 1.1 KEYS TO BUILDING & RETAINING PERSONAL RESILIENCE	
Maintain Physical Well-being Are you getting enough... ▪ Sleep ▪ Exercise ▪ Healthy food ▪ Time in nature ▪ Time to meditate and relax Are you limiting or eliminating: ▪ Caffeine ▪ Nicotine	**Fulfill Life Purpose Using Emotional Intelligence** Understand what you stand for, and maintain focus. Ask: ▪ What is my purpose? ▪ Why is it important to me? ▪ What values do I hold that will enable me to accomplish my purpose? ▪ What opportunities in my professional life do I have that help me achieve my life purpose? ▪ If I were successful beyond my wildest dreams, what would happen?
Manage Thinking Practice telling yourself: ▪ Challenges are normal and healthy for any individual or organization ▪ My current problem is a doorway to an innovative solution ▪ I feel inspired about the possibilities that did not exist before	**Harness the Power of Connection** Practice effective communication: ▪ Say things simply and clearly ▪ Make communication safe by being responsive ▪ Encourage people to ask questions and clarify if they do not understand your message ▪ Balance advocacy for your point with inquiring about the other persons' points ▪ When you have a different point of view, seek to understand how and why the other person believes what they do in a non-threatening way ▪ When in doubt, share information and emotions ▪ Build trust by acting for the greater good

Situational Analysis

Situational Analysis is the fourth core element of our leadership model. Though much of the work of building Innovative Leadership is based on an in-depth examination of your personal and professional experience, understanding the background or context of that experience is equally important. Consider that your experience isn't merely a collection of personal expressions, events, and random happenstance; rather, it is fundamentally shaped by the interplay of your individual attributes, shared relationships, and involved organizations.

Every moment of experience is influenced by a mutual interaction of self, culture, action, and systems. All four of these basic dimensions are fundamental to every experience we have. Situational Analysis involves evaluating the four-dimensional view of reality that is shown in Figure 1.5. This comprehensive approach ensures that all dimensions are aligned, ideally resulting in balanced and efficient action. We refer to these four dimensions as self, action, culture, and systems. This balancing without favoring elements is an important skill for innovative leaders.

At their peril, leaders can take a partial or narrow-minded approach to changing organizations. They over-emphasize systems change with little or no consideration to the culture or how their personal views and actions shape the content and success of the change. This multi-dimensional approach provides a more complete and accurate view of events and situations. Situational Analysis enables you to create alignment across the four dimensions on an ongoing basis.

Figure 1.5 Integral Model

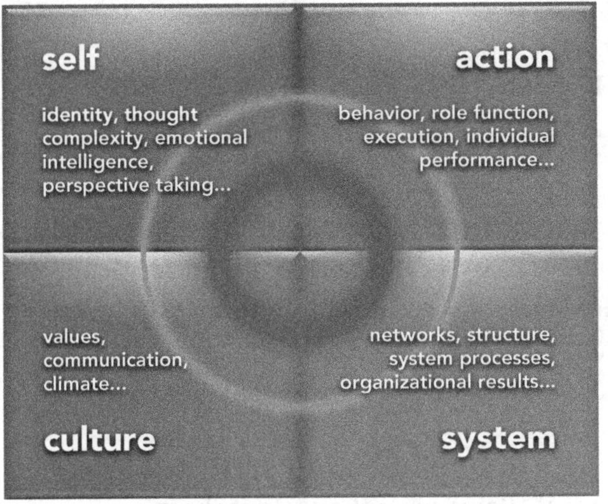

American-born philosopher, Ken Wilber, developed a conceptual scheme to illustrate the four basic dimensions of being, that form the backbone of experience. His Integral Model provides a map that shows the mutual relationship and interconnection among four dimensions, where each represents basic elements of human experience.

When you use Situational Analysis, you are cultivating simultaneous awareness of all four dimensions. Let's look at an example that will give you a more experiential description of how these dimensions shape every situation in your life.

Example: *"Visualize yourself walking into a hospital in the morning"*

Self *(Upper-Left Quadrant, "I")*: You feel excited and a little nervous about the big meeting today. Thoughts race through your head about how best to prepare.

Culture *(Lower-Left Quadrant, "We")*: You enter a familiar culture of shared meaning, values, and expectations that are communicated, explicitly and implicitly, every day. You understand how things work.

Action *(Upper-Right, "It")*: Your physical behaviors are obvious: walking, waving good morning, opening a door, sitting down at your desk, turning on the computer, and so on. Brain activity, heart rate, and perspiration all increase as the important meeting draws nearer.

System *(Lower-Right, "Its")*: Elevators, powered by electricity generated miles away, lift you to your floor. You easily navigate the familiar environment, arrive at your desk, and log on to the organization's intranet to check the latest patient records in the hospital's electronic medical record.

By applying Situational Analysis to organizational leadership as well as organizational change, you would be aware of the four dimensions as referenced above and when leading or changing one, you would consider the impact on the others. If you get promoted and want to be perceived differently, how will you behave in the situation above? What will be different in all four dimensions as you walk into the hospital?

To add to the complexity of diagnosing, analyzing situations, and the challenges that we face as leaders, our primary means of interaction is through language. Communication involves the leaders making meaning of what is happening based on the context as the leaders experiences it, translated into words that the listener then interprets and applies meaning to.

> ***Each of us at every moment is always already listening in a particular way, listening from...the particular set of values and concerns that constitute our identity. Our way of being and our understanding of the world, given by these values and concerns, constitute the listening that each of us always already is, the listening that determines the way the world occurs for us.***
>
> —Wiley W. Souba, *The Science of Leading Yourself: A Missing Piece in the Health Care Transformation Puzzle, 2013*

A crucial part of innovating leadership is developing your capacity to be aware of all dimensions of reality in any given moment and to identify misalignments or oversights and communicate them effectively. Even though you cannot physically see the values, beliefs, and emotions that strongly influence the way an individual colleague perceives himself/herself and the world, nor a group's culture, emotional climate, or collective perception, they still profoundly shape the vision and potential of leaders to innovate.

Situational Analysis is a tool of Innovative Leadership that allows you not only to make more informed decisions, but also helps you optimize performance within yourself, your teams, and the broader organization. The alignment of all dimensions is the key to optimizing performance.

Leadership Behaviors

Let's now shift focus to the actionable craft of leadership as observable skills and behaviors, and hard skills and their associated behaviors. This involves the fifth core element in our model (Figure 1.1), Leadership Behaviors. Leadership skills and hard skills are critical to success, and serve as objective performance measures of Innovative Leadership.

Hard skills fall into two primary categories: industry-related knowledge, skills, and aptitudes; and functional knowledge, skills, and aptitudes. Leadership skills can be evaluated by observable behaviors and result from knowledge, skills, and aptitudes specifically related to the craft of leadership.

We use the term *Leadership Behaviors* in this workbook when referring to leadership knowledge, skills, and aptitudes and the resulting behaviors. Both hard skills and Leadership Behaviors are critical to building Innovative Leadership; however, the balance between the importance of hard skills and Leadership Behaviors will shift as the leader progresses in the organization, with leadership skills and behaviors becoming increasingly important with career advancement.

Leadership Behaviors are important because they are the objective actions that leaders take to impact organizational success. We have all seen brilliant leaders behave in a manner that damages their organization and we have seen other leaders continually behave in ways that promote ongoing organizational success. Effective leadership behavior drives organizational success. Conversely ineffective Leadership Behaviors can drive organizational dysfunction or failure. Even the most functionally brilliant leader must demonstrate effective Leadership Behaviors to be successful when leading an organization.

An example of the need for both hard skills and Leadership Behaviors is a physician who is a hospital CEO. To be successful, this CEO must possess the hard skills in administration to understand how the hospital operates and the Leadership Behaviors to be able to effectively lead the people and the organization. If either of these sets of skills is missing, the leader and the hospital are at risk of failure. Early in his career, a mastery of administration set him apart from his peers. As he progressed into the senior leadership ranks and ultimately to the role of CEO, his use of Leadership Behaviors became his primary focus. While he never lost the need for hard skills, now he relies on his functional and leadership skills to guide his direction and action.

There are different ways to discuss leadership from a skills perspective as demonstrated by Peter Northouse in his book on leadership.

> ***There are several strengths in conceptualizing leadership from a skills [actions] perspective. First, it is a leader-centered model that stresses the importance of the leader's abilities, and it places learning skills at the center of effective leadership performance. Second, the skills approach describes leadership in such a way that it makes it available to everyone. Skills are behaviors that we all can learn to develop and improve. Third, the skills approach provides a sophisticated map that explains how effective leadership performance can be achieved.***
>
> —Peter G. Northouse
> *Leadership Theory and Practice, 2012*

As a leader, it is important to understand the key Leadership Behaviors important to you and your organization. With this understanding, you can determine where you excel and where you may want to refine your skills.

Leadership Competency Model

Competency-based approaches began in the 1970's. In 1973, David McClelland, a Psychologist and Professor at Harvard University, authored an impassioned article in The American Psychologist entitled, "Testing for Competence Rather than for 'Intelligence.'" In this article, Dr. McClelland proposed the idea of a competency-based assessment system for work and education, noting that the traditional intelligence-based assessments were both often scientifically invalid and poor predictors of success. That article ignited a movement that linked competencies in the form of knowledge, skills, abilities, and behaviors (KSABs) to human capital performance management and development.

A competency-based approach creates an integrated system that links KSABs to the hiring, performance management, promotion, and development of people. In order for the competency approach to be successful, the organization identifies the KSABs needed for a specific role, develops the competency, and ensures that the context or culture in which the competency is being used is integrated into the competency selection. The organization then works to ensure that the competency can be measured in a meaningful way.

While competency models certainly have their detractors, criticisms are most often aimed at the execution of the approach rather than the approach itself. This integrated, measurable, role-specific approach has several advantages over other developmental models. It is used extensively in the medical environment with competency guidelines and assessment of clinical skills.

While there are several effective leadership competency approaches, current competency models that measure and develop leadership KSABs often occur both too late in the leadership development process and are too tactical in nature. Due to the role-specific nature of most competency approaches, we generally find that new leaders get measured and developed as leaders only after they are already in leadership roles. This leaves a lot of opportunity for failure and heartache. Imagine an anesthesiologist who has been perfecting her or his clinical skills for several years but is now interested in moving into a leadership role within their hospital division. While this physician's intellect, knowledge of the hospital environment, and clinical skills are most likely at a very high level, this physician should have had the opportunity to develop their leadership KSABs BEFORE they attempted to move into a leadership position.

As significant, the KSABs required to be an effective resident or starting clinician only tangentially address the development of effective executive leadership skills. A mounting dossier of research points to developmental maturity as the key to effective leadership, especially as it relates to transformational leadership abilities. Researchers such as Ken Wilber, Susanne R. Cook-Greuter, Bill Torbert, and Terri O'Fallon define stages of developmental growth which they call Action-Logics (AL). These action logics are also the foundation for the Developmental Perspectives. They have transformed these ALs into a leadership development framework with measurable stages. The noteworthy difference between these ALs versus traditional KSABs is that ALs help define the leader's developmental lens rather than the leader's learned information. This is analogous to the difference between a competency that defines the use of a tool and a competency that defines the use of the hand using the tool. ALs have broader implications. We believe the ALs are an important foundation for the physician competencies described in the next chapter. While traditional KSABs like Executive Communication Skills and Situational Awareness tend to break down under conditions of stress and uncertainty, ALs tend to hold true under stress. This is due to how they define who the person has developed to become rather than what behaviors the person has learned to execute. Ultimately, both are critical for effective physician leadership.

The table below details seven transformational AL Leadership Competencies. Arising from the research on leadership developmental framework, these Action-Logic competencies serve as the roadmap for the planning, benchmarking, and measurement of effective transformational leaders. Each of the seven developmental competencies is measurable and can be effectively used to facilitate developmental growth.

TABLE 1.2: TRANSFORMATIONAL LEADER ACTION LOGIC COMPETENCIES AT STRATEGIST AND BEYOND This is a list of "Level 5" competencies focused on how you make sense of the world. The way you see the world drives how you behave. Very few people operate fully at this level, we are providing this list to help you see what Level 5 Leaders generally experience when they are operating at their highest potential.	
Professionally humble	***Cares about getting it right ahead of being right*** ■ Committed to personal and organizational mission as "north star" and focal point for where to invest energy in service of leaving a legacy ■ Cares more about the organization and the result than her/ his image ■ Freely, happily, and instinctively gives credit to others ■ Puts principles ahead of personal gain
Dogmatically committed to right action	***Is unstoppable and unflappable when on a mission*** ■ Has the dichotomous ability to be fully committed, hard driving, fully fo cused, and yet not experienced as either myopic or stubborn ■ Has the ability to 'stay the course' when under pressure
A 360 degree thinker	***Has the 'Balcony View' of the business*** ■ Innately understand the systems, constraints, perceptions, near term, long term, and secondary impacts of business strategy, decisions, and how to transform them to complete amazing results ■ Balances competing commitments of multiple constituents on a regular basis ■ Thinks in terms of systems, dialogues, and transformations when focusing on constraints and perceptions—consider the organizational context when making recommendations ■ Strong commitment to continual personal learning and building learning systems ■ Understands cross organizational impact—striving to understand the inter connection across multiple complex systems and make highly informed decisions considering implications across broader contexts
Intellectually versatile	***Has developed interests, expertise, and curiosity beyond the job and organization*** ■ Despite a devout commitment to the job and the organization; they are always interested and involved with areas beyond their comfort zones ■ Takes a special interest in political, national, and international developments ■ Use external interest to enhance legacy and provide balance in life

Highly authentic and reflective	***Is not constrained by personal appearance but is highly focused on personal behavior*** ■ Highly committed to personal growth and development and growing and developing others ■ Is so undefended and open to feedback it may be surprising ■ Seeks out discussions and feedback even in uncomfortable situations ■ Able to manage emotions in the most difficult situations: understand the impact and contagious nature of emotions so they develop skills to recognize them, manage/metabolize them and relate to others productively ■ Able to maintain perspective in times of stress, taking a long-term view and remaining vision focused, they are less challenged by difficult situations than others ■ Demonstrates emotional courage: willing to confront challenging situations ■ Continually looking for ways to enable the organization to improve its ability to meet its mission more efficiently and effectively
Able to inspire followership	***Has the special ability to connect with people at all levels of the organization to create a shared vision*** ■ Intuitively understands change, the steps to managing change, and how to help the organization overcome its resistance to change. Has an innate ability to diffuse conflict without avoiding or sidestepping the source of the conflict ■ Has a great ability to use humor effectively to put people at ease ■ Able to relate to a broad range of people and understand their motivators and stressors. Innately connect projects to the individual goals while working to overcome barriers ■ Able to provide valuable feedback to others in a manner that is supportive of growth and development of the recipient ■ Understands the complex nature of communication and is aware that what is said and what is heard are often different. Works to ensure the listener hears and understands the meaning of the words spoken
Innately collaborative	***Welcomes collaboration in a quest for novel solutions that serve the highest outcome for all involved*** ■ Seeks input from multiple perspectives: valuing diverse points of view ■ Creates solutions to complex problems by creating new approaches that did not exist, pulling together constituents in novel ways, creating broader and more creative alliances ■ Understands that in a time of extreme change, input from multiple stake holders with diverse points of view are required

Developing Innovative Leadership

Chapter two focuses specifically on Leadership Behaviors for physician leaders. Chapters three through eight walk you through the process of developing Innovative Leadership, specific to the medical field. Each chapter reflects one step in the development process and includes tools, templates, questions for reflection, and an example of a person who has completed the process. It is the comprehensiveness of this reflection, coupled with the exercises that will allow you to gain insight into yourself and your organization or practice. This insight is required to change yourself and your organization concurrently or to manage your internal change in the context of an organization that you cannot or do not want to change. It is important to reiterate that leadership development is an ongoing process, a journey. Upon completion of this process, you will be more effective; depending on your goals, you may still want to continue developing. Figure 1.6 shows the six steps.

Figure 1.6 Leadership Development Process

While this process appears linear, we have found that when leaders work through these steps, they often return to earlier parts of the process to clarify and sometimes change details they had originally thought were correct. The structure of our process will continue to challenge you to refine the work you have accomplished in prior tasks. Initial ideas are often good ones, but when you work with this tool over time, you will find new insight every step of the way. We encourage you to continue to test your ideas and feel comfortable going back in the process for further refinement.

The time you spend working on the workbook is an investment in your development. If you are engaging deeply in the process, it will likely take you three to six months or longer to complete. Through this time and thereafter, you will be refining and developing your leadership, hopefully informed by a strong commitment to improve and a passion for self-awareness and development. Remember that leadership is a journey. Whether managing either personal and organizational change, or internal change alone in the context of an organization that you cannot or do not want to change, reflection and thorough evaluation are required. This reflection will take time and is critical to your growth. We strongly encourage you to engage in the process with as much time and attention as possible. The value you ultimately take from this process is closely linked to the time you invest.

REFLECTION QUESTIONS

What innovative challenge does your hospital, practice, or health care facility face?

How does your organization support effective leadership for innovation and change?

In what ways would you consider yourself an innovative leader?

How do you personally connect with leadership and innovation?

Where are the opportunities for you to be an innovative leader?

What would make you and your organization more effective in leading innovation during a time of significant change in health care regulation?

If you were successful beyond your wildest dreams in becoming an effective leader, what would happen? Write the story as though it is a newspaper article with your name in the title of the article, "Dr. (Your Name) Has Been Celebrated as a Highly-Effective Health Care Leader."

CHAPTER 2

Developing an Innovative Physician Leader

Physician leaders are essential in today's medical sector for a variety of reasons, particularly because effective health care requires coordinated care delivery, and because health care is complex with multiple challenges, e.g., cost, access, and quality. Physicians must function in multiple roles, such as administrator, clinician, researcher, teacher, and leader (Schwartz & Pogge, 2000). The medical culture embraces autonomy, analytical thinking, and fast decision-making and is generally averse to unneeded ambiguity (McAlearney, Fisher, Heiser, Robbins, & Kelleher, 2005). Yet, physicians are trained to be "independent thinkers, skeptical scientists and self-reliant professionals" (Henochowicz & Hetherington, 2006, p. 183) and as "lone healers"

—Lee T, Harvard Business Review, April 2010

The professional norms and standards in physician training and the subsequent practice of medicine contribute to the lagging attention to leadership development. The traditional standpoint of medical leadership portrays physician leaders as strong, decisive, directive, and hierarchically-oriented. In contrast, a contemporary perspective of leadership has shifted to valuing emotional intelligence (and its embedded self-awareness), interpersonal relationships, and a participatory approach to successful leadership. Individuals trained as autonomous and independent agents therefore need to develop competencies in teamwork and collaboration. The current business models and approaches to leadership are new to health care organizations and to the education of physicians, but old models die hard.

—Hopkins, O'Neil, Bilimoria
Effective leadership and successful career advancement:
Perspectives from women in healthcare, 2006

Before moving into a description of important leader behaviors, we'll start our exploration of effective physician leadership with a true story.

"It was as if the lines were clearly and uncomfortably delineated. On the near side of a long, polished, mahogany table, everyone wore green scrubs; on the far side, everyone was in a suit. I remember that even the two female executives in the room were wearing blue suits that day."

Mary recalls working with Dr. Robert Francis (both pseudonyms) at a metropolitan hospital. Mary was the Chief Nursing Officer (CNO) and reported directly to Dr. Francis throughout her tenure as hospital president. "Staring at that beautiful table, I could see the reflection of everyone's facial expressions. They all looked tense through the red-brown mahogany haze. They had similar mixtures of anger, frustration, and distrust tempered by mixtures of dignity, elegance, and restraint—a constipated composure that everyone in the room shared; everyone except Robert." Mary looked up. "I remember this meeting in particular, because I was kind of scared. I know it seems silly. I had completed nursing school and had a Master's Degree, had practiced nursing for over ten years, had been promoted to CNO, and had two children; yet, I was still scared. I was way out of my comfort zone, and I had no idea how to work through this level of confrontation back then. I remember wondering how Robert was going to get out of this one!" Mary looked up and smiled.

"Robert was a very gifted heart surgeon," Mary reflected. "Robert's technical skills—even to other experienced cardiac surgeons—were impressive." As a leader, Robert effectively moved up the hospital chain of command from surgeon, to chief cardiac surgeon, to hospital president. "During his tenure as president, the hospital did incredibly well," said Mary. "Measures for quality, customer service, employee engagement, and financial position all improved. Robert was an amazing senior leader who never took himself too seriously. When Robert met with a patient or their family, he was just a man who cared. When he met with a nurse or colleague, he was just a man who cared. And when he met with us, he was just a man who cared about patients."

Mary began again, "I remember that the conference room was very light that day. Maybe even a little too bright. Someone had opened all of the blinds and the sun was at just the right angle to fill the room with bright white-blue light. Anyway, our Chief of Radiology had called the meeting. There were two different practicing radiology groups within our hospital system, and the two groups did not even pretend to respect each other. The hospital system was in the process of purchasing a Radiology PACS IT system, and the competing radiology practice wanted one kind of PACS system while our group wanted a different kind.

"On their side of the table sat our Chief of Radiology, two radiologists, two ER physicians, the head trauma physician, and two trauma suite nurses. On the other side of the table was Robert, the Vice President over our radiology services, the Director of Radiology, our hospital CFO, the hospital system CIO, and me. I don't think Clint Eastwood was there, but that was the only person missing in this showdown," Mary joked. "The radiology group was making a play to purchase its own PACS system and let the other hospitals use a second system. This would have increased the costs substantially. It also had clinical implications because if someone received a PACS X-ray at our hospital, but then was moved to another hospital in the system, the physicians at the other hospital would not be able to read the image from our PACS system." Mary paused. She looked as if she could feel the tension of that day all over again.

"As I said, everyone was tense—everyone, surprisingly, but Robert. He looked comfortable, engaged, completely unintimidated. Our Chief of Radiology began the meeting. Dr. Marc Gant was a very tall, slender, intense man with bright blue eyes. You didn't really worry about him losing control, yet it seemed like he had that type of impatience going on under the surface. Dr. Gant started the meeting by saying something like, 'Well, we all know why we are meeting today. We need to make a decision this morning about whether we really care about the clinical care in this hospital or if we have become medical robots that are slaves to the technology budget of the hospital system.'" Mary looked up at me and smiled, "The CFO and CIO looked like they were going to give birth."

"At that point in the meeting, Robert leaned in. He responded by saying something like, 'Marc, can we begin by reviewing what has happened, what is happening, and your proposal for the best way to move forward? I want to make certain that we are all aware of the same information.' Dr. Gant went on to explain the frustration with the selection process, the lack of collaboration between the two radiology practices, the problems with the PACS product the hospital system was reviewing, and his frustration with new clinical information systems in general. The scrubs side of the table joined in as Robert asked questions."

"After about thirty minutes of review, Robert asked, 'So if we joined the hospital system with this other product, is the biggest issue money, time, or patient care?' Marc answered, 'All three, and money is a big one. Our private ambulatory practices are currently using a mini-PACS and if we go with a new system, it will put us back to ground zero.' 'Got it,' responded Mary. 'Let's have our legal team look at how to properly address any Stark Law implications and Chris (the CFO) can look at how we might make this right financially.' Then Robert looked directly at Marc. 'I can't believe the hospital system would choose a PACS system that would compromise patient care. Frustrations aside, is that a fair statement?' Marc conceded the point. The rest of the meeting looked at how the selection process could be improved." Then Mary looked directly at me. I couldn't believe how well the meeting went. Where did Robert ever get the people skills to lead a room full of frustrated overachievers so effectively?"

Mary was describing Innovative Leadership under a highly developed leader. Mary watched as Robert exuded a calm, poise, and focus so natural that it seemed as if he were born with it. Robert, however, like most innovative leaders, hadn't been born with this resonant presence; rather, his presence was a skill developed over time. While Robert still had his moments of self-doubt, and was sometimes overwhelmed and often humbled, under most circumstances he was the most poised person in the room. His self-composure emitted a vibration so strong that everyone in the room became better, more collaborative, more creative—somehow *TRANSFORMED.*

At some point in your career, you most likely have had the same realizations as Mary had as you watched a truly resonant leader and said to yourself, "How will I ever become that good?" Or, conversely, you may have watched an underdeveloped leader stumble through a situation that you knew needed transformational skills and wondered, "How will I avoid being that inept?"

Robert's skill set included a long list of highly developed competencies that led to a transformational presence and innovative outcomes. You'll be developing these characteristics yourself, and the exciting news is that each of these five characteristics, when advanced, synergistically moves the other leadership characteristics forward. An analogy is that as an athlete becomes a stronger runner, she also becomes a stronger skier, or basketball player, or golfer.

Each skill that you develop will help you develop additional critical skills on the road to Innovative Leadership. The skill set that Robert had developed so effectively is embedded in the Innovative Leadership pyramid in the prior chapter. To help understand Robert's strengths and make them available to you, we selected six key competencies that are critical for physician leaders and are calling them out separately because there are specific areas that are important for your focus as a developing leader. These key competencies are the following:

- Technical knowledge
- Knowledge of health care
- Problem-solving prowess
- Effective communication
- Commitment to life-long learning
- Emotional intelligence

Even more good news, these competencies are not *INNATE*. If you come to this program with an open mind and a willingness to learn, you can DEVELOP all six of these competencies. We'll finish by defining each of these competencies.

Let's start with foundational knowledge. The physician leader needs to have a basic understanding of business practices referred to as *technical knowledge* and *knowledge of health care*, which relates specifically to understanding the fundamentals of how health care and medical practices operate. This foundational knowledge is then combined with specific leadership competencies that define the mindset and behaviors required of effective physician leaders.

Technical knowledge and skills (i.e., Operations, Finance and Accounting, Information Technology and Systems, Human Resources [including Diversity], Strategic Planning, and Policy) are required to understand how the health system or practice operates as an efficient and effective organization. Each of these elements is interconnected, and understanding this system serves as the foundation to both manage a practice and lead an organization. This competency includes:

- A working understanding of practice operations including: patient scheduling, staff scheduling, billing and collections, and the service delivery model.
- A working understanding of practice financial management: financial statements, practice operating results, practice financial analysis, understanding the revenue cycle, managing expenses, assessing measuring and controlling performance, internal controls and safeguards, budget formation and management, and other financial reporting.
- An understanding of the technology and systems required to operate the practice effectively, including staying current with process automation (latest tools to make the practice more efficient), addressing interoperability (interconnection) between offices and other partner organizations and/or between offices, addressing security issues, and addressing hardware concerns like what equipment do we maintain vs. outsource, and how do we track and manage the costs of technology.
- An understanding of foundational human resource (HR) practices and policies for hiring and retaining a loyal and effective staff, providing effective performance feedback, succession planning, and turnover management, staff evaluation, talent management, performance management, foundational HR policies, and diversity and inclusion. This category also includes consideration for leading practices that impact employee engagement and productivity.

- An understanding of how to conduct strategic planning and of your specific organization's strategic plan as well as the need to refresh and update the strategic plan intermittently. At a high level, this means evaluating the competition, evaluating your strengths and weaknesses compared to others in the market, identifying your differentiators based on where the market is now and where it is going, and creating a plan to accomplish strategic goals. It is critically important to be able to connect changes in the market to organizational differentiators that you integrate into the strategic plan and then build into ongoing scorecards and actions.

Knowledge of health care (i.e., of reimbursement strategies, legislation, regulation, quality assessment and management) is required to be an effective physician leader with regard to running the medical side of the practice. The leader and manager must understand the basic systems involved in running a medical practice in order to make solid decisions. While you do not need to be expert in each area, you do need to understand and be current on basic information and also understand the interconnections across the various elements. If a leader is to recommend changes to the organization and provide guidance, it is imperative to have a clear understanding of the impact those changes will have on the business and which "levers" to use to enact the changes.

- With ever-revising health care reimbursement policies, medical practice leaders need to continue to optimize the reimbursement from insurance companies and government payers and help patients with high deductibles receive necessary services. You need to understand the current and emerging approaches and to determine the approach that will enable the practice's financial success with optimal patient care.

- Legislation is changing at a dizzying pace and the practice's leaders must understand the impact of this legislation on the business and be able to make necessary changes to the practice operations to ensure compliance and long-term practice success.

- The regulations that states are confronting require substantial changes in the medical care delivery system, changes that are driven by private corporations and are sometimes in conflict with state policy. These changes demand quick regulatory responses that are only possible when decision-making is delegated to an agency, rather than being expressed only through the legislature. The states, through their policy power, have broad latitude to regulate the practice of medicine. Practice leaders must keep current on state regulations as well as legislation.

- Quality assessment takes many forms from health care documentation and transcription to the Press Ganey National Quality Measures Clearinghouse (NQMC) Medical Practice Survey whose "Overall Assessment" section is one of six sections that comprise the Medical Practice Survey. Each patient has a score for every question answered. For each patient, a section score is calculated as the mean of all the question scores in that particular section. Similarly, for each patient, an overall score is calculated as the mean of that patient's section scores. These assessments provide valuable information for practice effectiveness and efficiency, and leaders must have working knowledge of these instruments.

- Management is the ability to use solid technical knowledge from the first set of competencies above combined with knowledge of health care to manage a practice effectively. While not all physician leaders need to be effective practice managers, they need to have a solid understanding of the processes involved in running an effective practice and be able to provide solid thought partnership and thought leadership to those performing this role. Embedded within this competency is an understanding of change models. Because leadership frequently involves having vision and being able to engage others in effecting this vision, knowledge of how to be a change agent and how to orchestrate a change initiative is critical for the effective physician leader.

Problem-solving prowess (i.e., to resolve organizational challenges and manage projects). The effective leader understands the range of tools and methods available to solve problems and employs the most effective methods of process improvement to determine a solution. Solutions can range from those that are quick and directionally correct to those that are fully researched and have a high level of validity. It is important for you to know which approaches and tools are required and be able to respond accordingly. Effective problem-solving requires:

- Identifying problems
- Defining the root problem rather than solving symptoms
- Knowing a range of problem-solving and process improvement models and techniques and understanding which model or combination of models is best in which situation
    - Examples of such models include the "plan, do, check, act" cycle, and models that have come to health care form industry like "Lean," "Six Sigma," etc.
- Collecting data
- Using problem-solving models and change models to create a viable solution set
- Evaluating solution(s) for viability in the current situation
- Planning implementation
- Defining the project plan (i.e., developing and implementing a tactical approach)
- Managing and measuring implementation progress against the plan
- Evaluating success and taking corrective measures

Effective communication (in leading change in groups and in individual encounters, in negotiation, and conflict resolution) is the ability to connect deeply with others. We communicate in many ways, e.g., by e-mail, phone, text, and conversation. In the current technological era, we are often lulled into believing that because we have sent an e-mail, the message has been communicated and will be actionable. Nothing could be further from the truth and effective communication requires redundant and repeated communication involving multiple media—both by using technology and "in person," face-to-face communication.

Things—ideas, conversations, people—become intelligible to human beings through a process of linguistic distinctions. Speaking is less about transmitting words to someone else and more about participating in a "saying" that is a showing. "What unfolds essentially in language is saying as pointing…The saying grants those who belong to it their listening to language and hence their speech...[This saying] lets what is coming to presence shine forth…" (Heidegger, 1971). In using language as a "showing" that clarifies priorities or shows the way, good leaders help themselves and others "see" differently. This property of language, its ability to bring forth, out of the unspoken realm, new ideas and possibilities, will determine the future of our health care system and our world.

A key part of communication is recognizing the importance of using language effectively. "Language acts as a lens (a context) through which we "see" and understand life's challenges, other people, and ourselves. More relatedly, the way any leadership challenge occurs for us is through language. Making sense of our leadership challenges and crafting solutions is a linguistic process." (Souba, 2013) Leaders use language to convey meaning and influence others. (Souba, 2013)

Leadership often involves direct, personal communication and participation. Most of us do not stop to consider how effective we are at communicating, and many of us lack the advanced communication skills necessary to be truly successful. Like emotional intelligence, communication is embedded in all other areas. Each personality type has a preferred method of communication, and each type adapts that preference and builds on it to communicate. This idea of customizing one's communication and leadership style to the individual level of commitment and capability of those you are addressing has been called "situational leadership." Great leaders need to be aware of situations and capable of deploying a variety of leadership and communication styles to "meet people where they are." Factors to consider in developing effective communication skills are:

- Understanding the importance and emotional tenor of the conversation and responding accordingly. Ask and answer the question, "Is this a crucial conversation?" and, if the answer is "Yes," know how to conduct a crucial conversation.

- Understanding the priority to place on the conversation. How do I plan the timing and convey that I understand the importance?

- Understanding the level of trust required to effectively communicate this topic. Do I need to do anything to build trust and/or safety before engaging in a serious conversation with this person or group?

- Understanding how to address conflict in a productive and respectful manner.

- Understanding how to manage the "give and takes" of a negotiation that leaves both parties with a positive relationship—including finding creative solutions where both parties win rather than pure compromise.

- Understanding how to focus on issues and not people and to "be hard on issues and soft on people."

- Understanding the importance of language and use it effectively to not only convey information accurately but also change the mindset of others.

Life-long learning (in the context of a rapidly changing environment and the need for new skills to cope and manage). Life-long learning should include a continuous focus on building competence in the clinical and technical skills of being a current and effective physician in your selected specialty. Like Robert in the story above, your success as a physician leader will depend on gaining and maintaining the respect of your clinician colleagues for you as a doctor. Other critical areas of learning will include building knowledge, skill, and aptitude in the area of leadership skills. To be an innovative physician leader, you will need to remain proficient in all of the physician leadership competencies as well as develop in other areas of Innovative Leadership. It is this combination that will support your long-term success.

- Clearly define your professional goals and revisit them regularly. For example, in what dimension of your leadership do you wish to improve? How will you do so? How will you measure your success and by when would you expect to be successful? Asking these questions and being mindful about continuously getting better must become reflexes, because developing as an effective physician leader is a journey.
- Understand the market trends most likely to impact your skills and practice.
- Assess your performance against goals as well as against objective criteria such as a competency assessment using a generally accepted set of criteria such as The Leadership Circle 360 assessment or the Emotional Competency Inventory.
- Create a development plan to ensure that you build highest impact skills first.
- Track the impact of your development on your ability to accomplish your goals.

Emotional intelligence (EI, the ability to evaluate oneself and others and to manage oneself in the context of a group) is embedded throughout the Innovative Leadership model. The EI model has multiple competencies embedded within each of these four quadrants of self-awareness, self-management, relationship awareness, and relationship management. Examples of these component competencies include having an organizational service mindset, being optimistic, knowing how to build teams, knowing how to manage change, and exercising emotional self-control. Emotional intelligence incorporates many of the leadership competencies discussed above and is included as a foundational component to having resilience, having a Developmental Perspective, and modeling Leadership Behaviors. Each personality type relates to EI differently depending on its innate strengths and opportunities. Emotional intelligence is critical to leadership success and, by developing it, you will move forward in all other leadership areas.

Daniel Goleman, a psychologist and behavioral science journalist, popularized the term and developed related concepts in his influential book, *Emotional Intelligence* (1995). In *Working with Emotional Intelligence* (1998), Goleman explored the function of emotional intelligence on the job. According to Goleman, emotional intelligence is the largest single predictor of success in the workplace. Others have validated the importance of EI to success as a physician leader. Goleman describes emotional intelligence as "managing feelings so that they are expressed appropriately and effectively, enabling people to work together smoothly toward their common goals." According to Goleman, the four major skills that make up emotional intelligence are:

- Self-awareness
- Self-management
- Social awareness
- Relationship management

As an emotionally intelligent leader, you are aware of how situations impact you and effectively manage your responses. The more effective you are at managing your own emotions, the more you are able to tend to the impact you and various organizational situations have on those around you. Just like Robert in the story above, as a leader, you must remember that people look to you to see how you respond to situations. They take cues from your emotional reactions and from your actions—often more so than the words you use. So, if you are not managing your responses, you may impact others in unintended ways. The emotionally intelligent leader acts in ways that are consistent with the values that she espouses.

Summary

A highly effective physician will be characterized by the following competencies:

- Technical knowledge that allows you to understand the health care environment and the overall requirements of running an effective organization.
- Knowledge of health care that allows you to translate running an organization into running a medical practice by understanding and managing the key success indicators.
- Problem-solving prowess such that you are able to identify key problems and use a structured method to identify solutions and to manage their implementation.
- Effective communication in which you connect in a way that promotes a strong and an effective exchange of ideas and perspectives, and that allows everyone to move forward.
- Life-long learning that allows you to identify your key goals and match them with development activities that support your learning the key skills and abilities that are required to succeed.
- Emotional intelligence by which you manage your own emotions and your impact on others, as well as create strong healthy relationships with them.

Using this as a working definition for a physician leader, we will now look at how you can use the six-step Innovative Leadership Development Process to improve your effectiveness at this specific stage and also how you may guide others in their development.

Activity – Score yourself on a scale of one to five for each of the following categories. How are you currently performing? Understanding your current performance will help you identify where to focus your development activities.

Emerging Leader Job Requirements	Never	Rarely	Sometimes	Often	Almost Always
I demonstrate the **technical knowledge** that allows me to understand the overall requirements of running an efficient and effective practice as measured by financial performance as well as patient satisfaction and employee satisfaction.					
I understand how to run a successful **health care** practice in a way that allows me to respond quickly to the changing medical environment by understanding and managing the key success indicators.					
I have skill in **problem-solving** that allows me to identify key problems, and using a structured method, I identify solutions and manage their implementation.					
I use **effective communication,** connecting to others in a way that promotes a strong and effective exchange of ideas and perspectives and that allows everyone to accomplish their goals.					
I am committed to **life-long learning** that allows me to identify my key goals and match them with development activities that enable me to learn the key skills and abilities required to succeed.					
I demonstrate strong **emotional intelligence**. I manage my emotions and their impact on others effectively, and I create strong healthy relationships.					

CHAPTER 3

Step 1: Create a Compelling Vision of Your Future

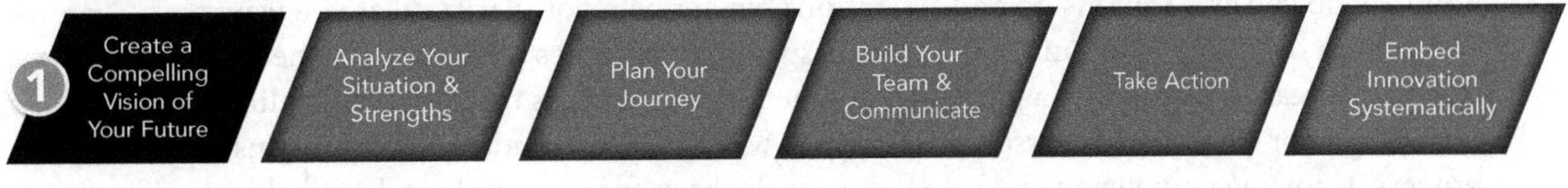

This workbook for physician leaders is designed to provide a step-by-step process to support you in developing your own Innovative Leadership capacity. The fieldbook, which serves as the foundation for this workbook, has been tested with a broad range of clients as well as hundreds of working adults participating in graduate programs.

The comprehensiveness of these exercises coupled with reflection exercises will give you the insight into yourself and your organization needed to make substantive personal change. While this process appears linear, we have found that when leaders work through these steps at their own pace and in their own way, they often return to earlier parts of the process to clarify and sometimes refine their answers. The structure of our process will continue to challenge you to refine the work you have completed in prior exercises. First ideas are often good ones, yet when you work with this tool you will continually find insight. We encourage you to continue to test your ideas and feel comfortable circling back for further refinement. This process is designed to give you a framework that you can apply in a way that is most effective for you (not a linear prescription). You may choose to pursue it in a linear fashion or more of an iterative fashion. What is most important is that you take the time to learn about yourself, examine your thoughts and behaviors but also below that to examine your own meaning making process. This is the "algorithm" that is critical for you to be able to access so you can update your own views as you learn and grow. This is the beginning of leading yourself.

"Leading ourselves begins by discovering who we are. "Becoming a leader," writes Warren Bennis, "is synonymous with becoming yourself. It is that simple. It is that difficult" (Bennis, 1994). This may sound like a cliché, but if we don't look at ourselves realistically, we will never learn from our experiences and we won't be able to crystallize what we truly care about and what we are willing to take a stand for. What it is to be human is inextricably linked to the way in which we lead. What gets in the way of (constrains) our being human also gets in the way of our leadership." (Souba, 2013)

This framework and these tools differ from many others in that they are more comprehensive; they direct you through an exploration that takes into account your unique, individual experience while simultaneously considering the groups and organizations to which you belong.

The first step of the six-step process—Create a Compelling Vision of Your Future—is a starting place for your development process by cultivating a sense of clarity about your overall vision, which can also be summarized as your direction and aspirations. The intention behind your aspirations fuels both personal and professional goals, as well as gives a sense of meaning to your life. When your actions are aligned with your goals, they drive the impact you create in the world at large.

As you move forward in the visioning process, we will guide you to begin thinking about individuals or groups who inspire or influence you.

Simply stated, your vision and aspirations help you decide where best to invest your time and energy. Clarifying vision and values help you define a manner of contributing to the world that authentically honors who you are. Your vision and aspirations further help you clarify what you want to accomplish over time. You can select the time span that resonates with you, whether a short-term—one to five years—or perhaps a longer-term time horizon, such as the span of your lifetime. After clarifying your own unique, personal vision, you will have the foundation for your ensuing change process. Knowing your vision and values creates the basis for your goals and can help you align your behavior with your aspirations.

As part of the envisioning process, it is important to consider the context of your leadership role, your hospital, practice, or health care facility. If you are clear about your personal vision, you can evaluate where and how you fit within that organization. On the other hand, if your vision differs significantly from what you do and how you work, the additional knowledge will guide you in finding a role that is a better fit (this transition may not happen in the short term). By knowing your vision and aspirations, you are equipped with information that helps you align the energy you invest with the work you do.

In addition to creating a well-defined vision, it is also important to be clear about your motivation. The combination of vision and desire is what will enable you to maximize your potential. Without sufficient desire, solid vision, and an understanding of your current capabilities, you are likely to struggle when progress becomes difficult.

Tools and Exercises

The exercises will guide you in identifying what is most important to you. First, you will define your future, and from that vantage point, clarify your vision and values. You will then consider how you want to focus your medical career, as well as the type and extent of the impact you want to have on the world.

It is important to note that many people who participate in this exercise will still not have a clearly articulated vision—this is because defining personal vision requires a great deal of introspection for many people. While some people grow up knowing what impact they want to make, for others, identifying a vision is a process of gradual exploration and will take more time and energy than completing a single workbook exercise. You will likely refine your vision as you progress through later chapters in the workbook, based on the information you learn about yourself. Because the envisioning process is iterative in nature—a process of self-discovery—the exercises in this book will serve as the foundation for a longer process that may take considerably more time to complete. It will likely change as you gain experience and as your introspective process matures.

Define Personal Vision

Follow the steps defined below:

Step 1: Create a picture of your future. Imagine at the end of your life looking back and imagining what you have done and the results you have created.

- What is the thing you are most proud of?
- Did you have a family? If so, what would they say about you?
- What did you accomplish professionally?
- What would your colleagues say about you?
- What would your friends say about you?
- What relationships were most fulfilling?

For the rest of this exercise, let that future person speak to you and help you set a path that enables you to look back with pride and say things like, "I feel fulfilled and at peace. I lived my life well."

Step 2: Write a story. Now that you have an image of what you will accomplish, write a brief story about your successful life. Include details about the questions above. Make it a story of what you went through to accomplish each of the results for the questions you answered. What you are trying to create is a roadmap for your journey that gives you greater insight into what you would want if you had the option to design your perfect life.

- Who helped you along the way?
- What did you enjoy about your daily life?
- Who was closest to you?
- What feelings did you have as you accomplished each milestone along the way?
- How did you mentor and contribute to the success of others?
- What did you do to maintain your health?
- What role did spirituality or religion play in your journey?
- What job did you have?
- What role did material success play in your life?
- What type of person were you (kind, caring, driven, or gracious)?

Step 3: Describe your personal vision. Given the story you have written and the qualities you demonstrated as a person, write a two to five sentence life purpose statement about your highest priorities in life and your inspirations. This statement should capture the essence of how you want to live your life and project yourself.

An example - *I develop myself to my greatest capacity and help others develop and thrive in all aspects of their lives. I am wise, conscious, compassionate, and courageous, and contribute to making the world a better place through my actions.*

Step 4: Expand and clarify your vision. If you are like most people, what you wrote is a mixture of selfless and self-centered elements. People sometimes ask, "Is it all right to want to be covered in jewels, or to own a luxury car?" Part of the purpose of this exercise is to suspend your judgment about what is "worth" desiring, and to ask instead which aspect of these visions is closest to your deepest desire. To find out, before going on to the next one, ask yourself the following question about each element: If I could have it now, would I take it?

Some elements of your vision don't make it past this question. Others pass the test conditionally: "Yes, I want it, but only if..." Others pass, but are later clarified in the process. As you complete this exercise, refine your vision to reflect any changes you want to make.

After defining and clarifying your vision, it is time to consider your personal values. The combination of these two exercises will help you create the foundation of what you want to accomplish and the core principles that guide your actions as you work toward your vision.

Checklist for Personal Values

Values are deeply held views of what we find worthwhile. They come from many sources: parents, religion, schools, peers, people we admire, and culture. Many go back to childhood; others are taken on as adults. Values help us define how we live our lives and accomplish our purpose.

Step 1: Define what you value most. From the list of values (both work and personal), select the ten that are most important to you—as guides for how to behave, or as components of a valued way of life. Feel free to add any values of your own to this list.

TABLE 3.1: PERSONAL VALUES CHECKLIST

- Achievement
- Advancement and promotion
- Adventure
- Arts
- Autonomy
- Challenge
- Change and variety
- Community
- Compassion
- Competence
- Competition
- Cooperation
- Creativity
- Decisiveness
- Democracy
- Economic security
- Environmental stewardship
- Effectiveness
- Efficiency
- Ethical living
- Excellence
- Expertise
- Fame
- Fast living
- Fast-paced work
- Financial gain
- Freedom
- Friendships
- Having a family
- Health
- Helping other people
- Honesty
- Independence
- Influencing others
- Inner harmony
- Integrity
- Intellectual status
- Leadership
- Location
- Love
- Loyalty
- Meaningful work
- Money
- Nature
- Openness and honesty
- Order (tranquility/stability)
- Peace
- Personal development/learning
- Pleasure
- Power and authority
- Privacy
- Public service
- Recognition
- Relationships
- Religion
- Reputation
- Security
- Self-respect
- Serenity
- Sophistication
- Spirituality
- Stability
- Status
- Time away from work
- Trust
- Truth
- Volunteering
- Wealth
- Wisdom
- Work quality
- Work under pressure
- Other: __________

Step 2: Elimination. Now that you have identified ten values, imagine that you are only permitted to have five. Which five would you give up? Cross them off. Now cross off another two to bring your list down to three.

Step 3: Integration. Take a look at the top three values on your list.

- How would your life be different if those values were prominent and practiced?
- What exactly does each value mean? What do you expect from yourself, even in bad times?
- Does the personal vision you've outlined reflect those values? If not, should your personal vision be expanded? Again, if not, are you prepared and willing to reconsider those values?
- Are you willing to create a life in which these values are paramount and help an organization put those values into action?

Now, which one item on the list do you care most about?

Putting Vision into Action

After defining and clarifying your vision and values, the next step is to reflect on how to put them into action. You will consider the things you care about most as well as your innate talents and skills to determine what about your current life you would like to refine or change. You are probably passionate about specific interests or areas within your life; if you're really fortunate, you will have opportunities to participate in one or more of those areas.

You likely have passions that will always remain in the realm of hobbies. The purpose of this exercise is to consider how best to incorporate your passion into your profession and the goal is to move closer to identifying your passions and expressing them in as many areas of life as possible.

In our experience, part of figuring out how we want to focus is paying attention to what you find profoundly interesting. Those interests simply reveal themselves in the course of your daily interaction with peers and colleagues, and quite frequently at professional functions. They are reflected in whatever you find yourself reading; they even display themselves in the context of more casual occasions and are often seen in activities shared among friends.

This type of exercise appears very simple on the surface, but may be something you revisit annually in order to refresh what is genuinely important to you. We find that revisiting allows you to nurture a sense of continual clarity about your direction and iteration provides a mechanism for clarifying your direction as you grow and develop. With everything you try (false starts and all), you will discover a deeper truth about yourself that moves you closer to your most authentic passions. Some of those passions will be incorporated into your career; other passions shape your personal life.

Exercise: Putting Vision into Action

Step 1: Identify your foundation. Answer the three questions below by compiling a list of responses to each.

- What are you passionate about? This will come from the prior exercise and should now be relatively concise.
- What meets your economic needs?
- What can you be great at?

*Note: your answers to these questions should reflect your values from the Personal Values Checklist.

Step 2: Review and identify overlap. Review your answers and identify the overlaps.

Step 3: Harvest the ideas. Based on the overlaps, do you see anything that might be incorporated in what you do or how you work? This could mean adding an additional service within your profession or allocating a portion of your work time to a project that aligns with your values.

An example of this is a client who, based on significant reflection, learned he valued giving back to the community in a way that he was not doing at the time. He was the CEO of a technology firm and though born and raised in India, his passion was offering computer training for returning U.S. veterans. Even though he maintained the job of CEO, he added a community support function into his business. His passion for service to the community and professional skills afforded him the ability to follow his passion and still run a successful business. In the process of following his passion, he is building the workforce in his community and building his reputation as a civic leader and successful entrepreneur.

Vision-Based Actions

Innovative Leadership Reflection Questions

To help you develop your action plan, further clarify your direction using the reflection questions below. "What do I think/believe?" reflects your intentions. "What do I do?" reflects your actions. "What do we believe?" reflects the culture of your organization (i.e., work, school, community), and "How do we do this?" reflects systems and processes for your organization. This exercise is an opportunity to practice Innovative Leadership by considering your vision for yourself and how it will play out in the context of your life. You will define your intentions, actions, culture, and systems in a systematic manner.

Table 3.2 contains an exhaustive list of questions to appeal to a broad range of physician leaders and you will likely find that a few of these questions best fit your own personal situation. Focus on the questions that seem the most relevant. We recommend you answer one to three questions from each category.

TABLE 3.2: QUESTIONS TO GUIDE THE LEADER AND ORGANIZATION

What do I think/believe?

- How do I see myself in the future? What health care trends do I see around me that impact this view? Have I considered how these trends impact the way I want to contribute?
- How does my view of myself impact me? Am I inspired by my vision? Terrified?
- How do I see myself within the larger health care environment? This can range from my personal work environment to the broader health care environment.
- How do I gather input from key stakeholders to incorporate into my vision?
- After doing the exercises, what is my vision?
- After doing the exercises, what are my values? What do I stand for? What do I stand against?
- What are the connections between my organizational vision and my personal mission, passion, and economic goals?

What do I do?

- How do I research trends that will impact health care so I can understand my future placement and how to navigate potential transitions?
- How do I synthesize competing goals and commitments to create a vision that works for me in the con text of the communities I serve (family, friends, work, and community)?
- How do I develop my vision taking into account greater economic and government regulatory environment?
- What do I tell others about my vision? Do I have an "elevator speech"? Is it something I think is inspirational?
- When others observe me living my vision and values, what observable behaviors do they see?

What do we believe?

- How does my personal vision fit within the larger context of my family, my community, my professional role?
- How do I create a shared belief that my vision will help the organization succeed within the larger community and also help the community succeed?
- What do we believe we stand for as a hospital system or practice? How should we behave to accomplish what we stand for (guiding principles/values)? Do my values align with the organizational values?
- How do I reconcile differences between my values and those of my organization? How will these differences impact my ability to develop toward my vision and goals?

How do we do this?

- How do I monitor the organization's impact on my vision? How do I honor my vision when helping de fine/refine the organizational vision?
- What is our process for defining/refining changes to our shared vision for the organization and other systems I function within? What is our process for clarifying and documenting our values? How do I en sure that my values are aligned with our guiding principles?
- Who gives me feedback on their perspective of my progress? How often? What form would I like this feedback to take?
- What measures help me determine progress toward my vision and values? How do I track and report progress toward these goals? Is my behavior supporting the organizational goals? Are the organizational goals supporting my goals?

Introduction to Susan

To support your success in this workbook, we provide an example of Susan, whose character is representative of a mid-level multiple physician leader. This composite was developed by the authors, drawing on their experiences and those of their colleagues in various medical institutions. Susan tests as a "level 5 leader," (reference to advanced leadership capability from *Good to Great*) so her answers reflect that level of thinking and perspective taking. Her completion of many of the exercises, work sheets, and reflection questions gives you an example of how a successful physician leader might use this process. While Susan's answers reflect those of a physician leader in a university setting, this book is also designed to support physicians working in hospitals and private practice.

In her upper-40s, Susan was recently appointed as the chair of the department of internal medicine at a large academic medical center. She is using the workbook to help her identify the leadership changes that are needed for her to succeed in her new role.

Susan first joined the medical center as an assistant professor of cardiology. She completed her residency and fellowship at a prestigious east coast university medical center. After interviewing for both private practice and academic positions, she ultimately chose to relocate and begin her career at this large midwestern university because it offered a chance to further develop her research interests and to build a clinical practice devoted specifically to the care of patients with congestive heart failure. The geographic location was also a great fit for her husband's career and had the added benefit of being close to family members.

Susan devoted herself to her new position, achieving successful funding with a competitive grant award for her research in cardiomyopathy. She began to build her clinical practice, focusing specifically on heart failure patients. At the same time, she was asked to join various division and department level committees. She was asked to lecture in the pre-clinical medical student program, and ultimately asked to assume directorship of the cardiovascular curriculum for the first year medical students. Between her research, her burgeoning practice and her teaching responsibilities, she had little free time, but she found the variety and intensity of her work exhilarating. Five years after joining the department she was successfully promoted to the position of associate professor.

By this time, she had solid funding and was gaining national recognition for her clinical research on ventricular assist devices. In addition to supervision of her research team and manuscript preparation, she began to travel more extensively to present at national and international meetings. Her clinic became a regional resource, and other cardiologists referred their most complex and challenging cases. She continued to work with students, residents, and fellows in her clinic and was a respected and well-liked teacher. Ultimately she won the "Teacher of the Year" award from the graduating medical student class. She was asked to lead the development of a newly-endowed center of excellence in cardiomyopathy and heart failure. Between her research, teaching, and clinical work, she was the veritable "triple threat." Ten years after her hire, she was promoted to full professor, joining the relatively few other women at that rank in the cardiology division.

For the next several years, Susan continued as a respected member of the cardiology division. She enjoyed relative autonomy to pursue her research and clinical interests. She had a solid track record of research funding, and she was granted an endowed chair in cardiology at her institution. Periodically she received calls from colleagues and recruiters asking her to consider leadership positions at other universities. Initially she did not consider any of these seriously, in part because of her satisfaction with her current position and in part because of geographic constraints based on her family's needs. However, she began to realize that she felt complacent in her current position. She missed the invigoration of her earlier career when she was developing a center of clinical excellence, making novel discoveries, and mentoring students and trainees. When the chairman of internal medicine at her own institution announced plans to retire, Susan decided that the timing and opportunity were right. She sent a letter of interest which was received with enthusiasm by the search committee and dean. After an abbreviated national search, Susan received unanimous support and was named the department chair of internal medicine. Susan is the first woman to lead the department, which comprises over 400 faculty members in twelve different divisions. During her onboarding, Susan became aware of the magnitude of the different issues facing the department and realized that she would need astute leadership skills to succeed in her new position.

Now that we have read Susan's introduction, it is time to review her vision:

- Maintain personal accountability, humility, integrity, and honesty with myself and others
- Treat others with beneficence, compassion, and respect
- Recognize that my potential for personal growth, transformation, and lasting impact are infinite
- Leave a legacy of education, health, and well-being within my community and beyond

Three Core Values

- Compassion
- Excellence
- Effectiveness

Susan answered reflection questions from each category. She shares these answers with you because reflection is one of the more important skills that all leaders must develop. One important element of this workbook is that as a developing leader you have the opportunity to glimpse inside the thought process of a successful physician leader. It is rare that many leaders share their inner thoughts and feelings, and it's valuable for you to see how others approach these questions.

REFLECTION QUESTIONS

What do I think/believe?

- ***How do I see myself in the future?***

I see myself as a person who can significantly contribute to the growth and innovation of the department and as someone who has the vision to assure that the department is well-positioned to thrive in the changing health care environment. I face challenges head-on, am decisive, action-oriented, and stay focused on long-term goals. I also value the worth of individuals and am compassionate, fair, and respectful of diverse opinions. I place a priority on mentoring students, staff, and junior colleagues. I value the many communities to which I belong, as evidenced by my volunteer and service work. I will use these skills and values to continue to contribute to the field of medicine by continuing my clinical practice and continuing to prepare medical students. Ultimately as I look back over my career in education and medicine, I hope to leave a legacy of patients healed, families treated with compassion during the healing process, and students who have moved forward to become highly principled, compassionate, and effective physicians. In addition to my work, I hope to maintain a happy marriage and strong community ties. Beyond my work, I care deeply about the broader social systems that contribute to health and healing, and how they contribute to illness. What I mean by this is that I hope to make an impact on our social systems so that we have healthier communities and thereby a higher quality of life for everyone. I expect my research to contribute to not only healing the sick but also maintaining health within communities.

- ***How does my view of myself impact me? Am I inspired by my vision?***

If I live true to my vision, I know that I will assuredly reach my personal and professional goals. I view myself as someone who can contribute significantly to the organization because of the wisdom and perspective that I have gained through my unique personal journey and experiences. I am aware of my strengths and talents as well as my fallibilities. I also recognize my tendency to underplay my strengths and magnify my weaknesses. I realize that this exaggerated humility can diminish my confidence, make me risk adverse, and potentially constrain my progress as a leader. This level of self-awareness provides me with a foundation for personal development.

I am highly inspired by my vision—it guides my actions. I am committed to leaving a legacy through my work and community involvement. Additionally, I experience great joy from my family time. If I am able to accomplish my vision, I believe I will be able to say I have lived my life well.

What do I do?

- ***How do I tell others about my vision? Do I have an 'elevator speech'? Is it something I think is inspirational?***

  Explaining my vision to others, and more importantly, doing so in a way that inspires and engages them, is quintessential to the development of a shared vision and a synchronous, high-performing team. It helps to 'think big.' In describing my own research, for example, if I launch into the granular details of my work on postpartum cardiomyopathy and its clinical relevance, I may quickly lose an audience. On the other hand, if I start by saying that with my research, I am working to assure that every mother will see her child's first birthday and many more, then I've shared my vision and long-term goal in a way that the listener can understand and relate to. When successful, there is a transfer of energy and the beginning of a shared mental model and synergistic collaboration. It still takes work for me to manage my communication this way, but I realize that the payback can be enormous. This vision inspires me, and I believe that I will inspire others when I share it.

- ***When others observe me living my vision and values, what observable behaviors do they see?***

  An important developmental step for a physician is the formation of professional identity, how a doctor thinks of him/herself as a doctor. Professional identity is intrinsic, but is manifested by actions and behaviors, including professionalism. When others see me living my vision, I want them to see accountability and honesty, humility, integrity, and compassion as I lead in a manner that strives for the "good of the whole." On a personal basis, I want others to feel that they are valued, supported, respected, and treated fairly. On an organizational level, I want my work to demonstrate effectiveness and excellence.

What do we believe?

- ***How do I create a shared belief that my vision will help the organization succeed within the larger community and also help the community succeed?***

  Buy-in from all levels of the internal organization is critical to the success of the department and beyond. When an organization is united and striving toward the same purpose and goal, there is maximal synergy and productivity. When there is a lack of shared vision and motivation, the organization is at risk for becoming inefficient, fragmented, and fraught with internal conflict. For these reasons, "selling" my vision, first to key stake-holders, and ultimately to all members of the department, is an important early goal in my leadership. When key stakeholders such as chiefs and other leaders are aligned, they will serve as strong ambassadors to further amplify and message my vision. Individuals need to understand, "What's in it for me?" and the vision needs to reach that individual level. From an external standpoint, everyone loves a winner. When other departments, medical center leadership, and the dean see a productive, effective, high-performing department committed to excellence, they are more likely to seek collaboration, dedicate resources, and support new programs. The process of creating a shared vision will start with initial individual discussions where I discover the individual perception of the group vision. Depending on what I learn, I will then create an approach to group discussion(s) in which we ensure that the overall group is aligned with me and with one another. I hope that we are already close to being aligned, and I will confirm or disconfirm this assumption during the process.

- ***What do we believe we stand for as an organization? How should we behave to accomplish what we stand for (guiding principles/values)? Do my values align with the organizational values?***

As an organization, we stand for delivering high-quality, humanistic, and personalized health care in an efficient and compassionate and excellent manner. We also stand for creating the future of medicine through innovation, investigation, and translation of new discoveries and treatments from the bench to the bedside. Additionally, we have an important mission to educate and train the next generation of health care providers. As a department, we need to collectively succeed in all three realms, and to meet benchmarks that demonstrate that success. We need individuals who are experts in each (not all) of these areas, and who are supported in their efforts and valued for their contributions. We also need to establish a conceptual framework of collaboration and teamwork. Individual contributions, much like the proverbial stone soup, combine to create a high-performing and dexterous team, and teams combine to create a dynamic, productive, and multi-faceted department.

How do we do this?

- ***How do I monitor the organization's impact on my vision? How do I honor my vision when helping define/refine the organizational vision?***

In accepting the chair position, I have already confirmed that my vision is aligned with the organization. As I reflect, I realize that I have been intrinsically aware of the alignment, and this congruence has contributed to my long tenure at the institution. However, organizational visions do transform over time and in response to external forces. Therefore, as I was considering the chair position, I met with key college, medical center, and university leaders to assure that the organizational vision(s) were consistent and compatible with my personal vision. This is an important premonitory step for any individual considering a leadership position within an organization. As I begin my role as chair, it will be important to be aware of the changes and shifts in the organizational vision, and to be cognizant of how my own leadership will need to continually readjust to adapt to the larger vision and to remain directionally consistent. At the same time, my core values will remain strong, and will always guide the means by which I lead the department. There are many ways to reach an agreed upon destination, and my personal guiding principles and values will help define the unique pathway of my leadership.

- ***What processes and measures alert us to urgency in our system that we need to tend to? What are the early warning signs?***

There are many "red flags" that signal distress in an organization. There are several factors that need to be on my radar as a chair. The first is a performance dip. Unhappy employees are less productive employees. When individuals do not feel supported, valued, acknowledged, and respected, motivation lags and a performance dip ensues. This may be manifest by a drop in clinical productivity, reduction in research grants and publications, or by less favorable evaluations from students and house staff. On an individual basis, this can be a warning sign of burnout or other personal difficulty. On a department level, this can reflect systemic distress related to culture or leadership. As I move forward in my leadership position, it will be important for me to monitor individual and group performance, to acknowledge when suboptimal performance measures are a bellwether for future serious problems, and to look for root causes and solutions. The second, more serious flag is an increase in attrition. While some degree of attrition is natural, the departure of larger numbers of individuals may be a warning bell. It is not just about numbers. For instance, failure to retain certain demographic groups (such as women faculty, research scientists, clinical experts, educators, etc.), or specific subspecialists signifies a need to look at the organizational culture, reward system, and needs of those groups. I recognize that as a leader, I will need to systematically monitor certain internal indicators in order to take a positive and proactive approach.

I will work with our HR representative to create a scorecard that I will monitor quarterly. Additionally, we will conduct an annual employee engagement assessment. There are several that are available, and we have not yet selected one. I am leaning toward a model that evaluates individual satisfaction, group satisfaction, leadership quality, innovation, and creativity. I believe this comprehensive approach will maximize the information we get and allow us to be proactive in continuing to build and maintain an organization that supports our overall goals.

Creating a Compelling Vision for Yourself

Now that you have read Susan's personal narratives, it is time to complete the exercises and answer the questions for yourself. We encourage you to complete all of the exercises as they establish a strong foundation for your personal vision, values, and course of action; so, be patient and give yourself time to explore your hopes and dreams as authentically as possible. You will know you've completed this step and are ready to move to the next when you feel you have created a vision and set of values that truly inspire you.

Throughout this chapter, we have discussed exercises that will help you clarify your life direction and create a compelling vision for your own life and work. The next chapter focuses on assessing where you are now in your career and personal development.

Define personal vision and values

What do I think/believe?

What do I do?

What do we believe?

How do we do this?

CHAPTER 4

Step 2: Analyze Your Situation and Strengths

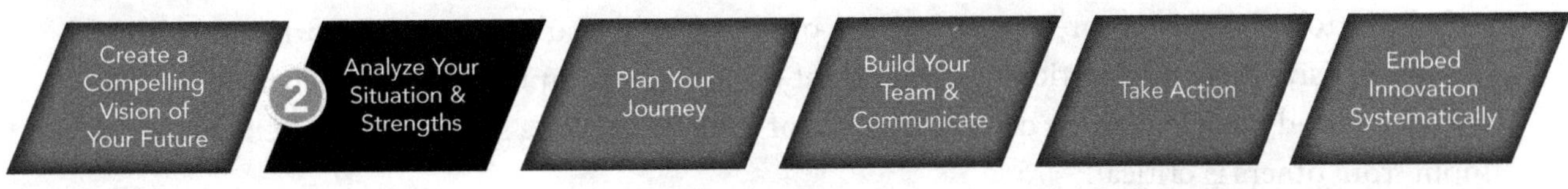

Now that you have developed (or refined) your vision, it is time to examine your strengths and development opportunities. This step will help you refine and clarify those strengths and weaknesses using standard assessment tools. You will then decide which areas you would like to improve by building on what you already do well and addressing weaknesses. We recommend using a general guideline that focuses eighty percent of your effort on building your existing strengths and twenty percent on addressing weaker areas. Although this is a general approximation, the 80/20 rule is a directional one stemming from the belief that you are already successful and have simply taken the opportunity to further advance and refine your capabilities. In the rare case that a successful physician finds serious deficiencies, we encourage you to ignore the rule of thumb and seek the required resources.

It is important to combine your vision with a firm understanding of your current performance, abilities, and personality type. The data will help you become more aware of your strengths and weaknesses, and also clarify how others see you. The combination of information will help you determine the gap between your current state (based on assessment data) and your vision.

Many people have a higher capacity than they are able to use at work. This could be caused by working in a role or organization that does not use your full abilities. Even as a physician, you may find you are filling a role that does not use the full range of your skills or even interests. When you begin taking assessments, it will be important to get information from a broad range of sources to ensure that you have a clear and accurate picture of your true capacity.

Assessment Tools

One of the primary ways to help you understand your current development and performance is by using a combination of assessments to measure your current skills and abilities along with your personality style and Developmental Perspective.

This should allow you to identify the gap between your present state and what you need in order to fulfill your vision.

Several good assessments are available. The tools we suggest have been used extensively and are recommended with a high degree of confidence. We find that each provides vital information in helping to convey a comprehensive picture of strengths, weaknesses, and opportunities. This comprehensive picture is particularly important because one's limitations are often hidden and therefore need pointing out by others. The role of feedback using a suite of assessments that includes input from others is critical.

These assessments are aligned with the five elements of Innovative Leadership discussed in chapter one. Some are expensive and require a skilled coach to interpret them; however, we know this option is not practical for everyone. Metcalf & Associates has created a free online assessment that, while it does not replace the detailed assessments recommended below, it does offer a high-level view of your Innovative Leadership and can indicate key areas of focus. It can be accessed by going to www.metcalf-associates.com/innovative-leadership-assessment.html.

The tools we use to help develop innovative physician leaders are:

Leader Type Assessment - Enneagram

We recommend using the Enneagram first and foremost to discover your own personality type and, as appropriate, to determine the types of those with whom you interact. The Enneagram is used for personal growth, relationships, therapy, and in the business world as an indicator of an individual's primary personality type. The *Riso-Hudson Enneagram Type Indicator* (version 2.5) provides a reliable, independently scientifically validated tool for that purpose. Finding your type is not the final goal, but merely the starting place for working with our system, and embarking on a fascinating and rewarding journey of self-reflection.

The Enneagram helps you to see your own personality dynamics more clearly. Once you are aware of the importance of personality types, you see that your own style is not equally effective with everyone. One of the Enneagram's most useful lessons is how to move from a style of interacting in which others are expected to mold themselves to your way of thinking/values to a more flexible style in which you act from an awareness of the strengths and potential contributions of others. By doing so, you help others become more effective themselves—and as a result, harmony, productivity, and satisfaction are likely to increase (source: www.enneagraminstitute.com/practical.asp). The Enneagram is an inexpensive assessment that is available online and does not require a certified coach to interpret.

Developmental Perspective - MAP

We recommend the Maturity Assessment Profile (MAP) to evaluate Developmental Perspective. Dr. Susanne Cook-Greuter developed this assessment to describe developmental perspectives as part of her Ph.D. at Harvard University. It is widely considered one of the most rigorously validated, reliable, and advanced assessment tools used to evaluate adult leadership development. Participants taking the assessment complete thirty-six sentence stems about various topics. The freeform response format allows test takers to provide a wide range of information which gives the scorer ample data to evaluate varying developmental features along three main lines: cognitive complexity, emotional affect, and behavior. The combination of the three allows the scorer to determine the action logic, or how people tend to reason and respond to life. It is critical for you to be completely open and honest when taking this assessment in order for there to be sufficient data to provide an accurate score. The MAP assessment is available through Pacific Integral (www.pacificintegral.com) or Susanne Cook-Greuter (www.cook-greuter.com). This assessment requires a coach to interpret the data and comes with a detailed report explaining the developmental levels and the perspectives each offers.

Resilience Assessment

Metcalf & Associates created a basic tool to help you assess your attitudes and practices that help support resilience, and identify areas where you can further build your capacity. It is based on fundamental stress management research including the characteristics that support "stress hardiness," a concept pioneered by Suzanne Kobasa. This assessment can be found at www.metcalf-associates.com/resilience-assessment-tool.html. This tool is free of charge, does not require a coach to provide feedback, and is also not validated. It provides useful information to support your personal awareness.

Situational Analysis

We do not have a specific tool to recommend for Situational Analysis. We suggest you use your score from the Innovative Leadership assessment at the beginning of this book as a rough indicator of development opportunities you may have in this area. Taking a 360° assessment also helps you determine how your specific behaviors align with the expectations of others within your hospital system or practice.

Leadership Behaviors - The Leadership Circle Profile (LCP) Competency-Based 360° Assessment

It is important for a leader to have an accurate view of what others see in order to be able to make appropriate changes and gauge the impact of these changes. This tool looks specifically at a set of well-researched and validated leadership behaviors that are key levers to drive success. It not only allows you to identify possible behavioral changes, it can also help you improve your self-awareness by specifically understanding how others see you. It is this ability to see what others see that will allow you to target your behavioral changes and fine-tune your effectiveness. The Leadership Circle is available at www.theleadershipcircle.com and requires a certified coach to administer and provide feedback.

It is important to note that how others perceive you is, in part, based on their own values and overall view of the world. Interpreting that data can be just as much an art as scientific inference. Rather than taking such feedback at face value, we suggest trying to understand those evaluations as well as the culture of the organization. For example, if an individual is very results-oriented in a culture that prefers collaboration, that individual may be perceived as having a negative disposition—controlling, driven, and autocratic. Another organization with a culture that is more aligned with a results-driven approach may perceive that very same individual as being extremely positive—achieves results, vision-focused, and system-oriented. Part of development and effectiveness is finding an organization that is aligned with your leadership style, as well as a culture that can support your potential to grow.

Physician Leadership Competency Assessment

Physician leadership competencies are explained in chapter two. There are several assessment instruments that physician leaders can use to gain a better understanding of their current level of capability and readiness to fulfill the demanding role of physician leader. The Physician Competencies Inventory (GCI) (The Kozai Group, Inc., 2008), the Physician Mindset Inventory (GMI) (Javidan et al., 2007), and the Physician Executive Leadership Inventory (GELI) (Kets de Vries et al., 2004), are three well-known assessment instruments utilized in physician leadership development. Each focuses on different, specific sets of physician leadership competencies. We recommend you consider using one of these assessments to specifically test your physician leader behaviors and competencies.

Future Projections

We find that reading futurist publications for specific industries is very helpful. The role of the futurist is to evaluate current trends and build possible scenarios for how the future might unfold. By building on our capacities for leadership, you can use these scenarios as part of our planning process to provide insight into overall societal trends to ensure you are well prepared for the potential impact of ever-changing business conditions, and to suggest imminent scenarios that help you navigate those trends effectively.

Several organizations provide very effective views into the future. One that we regularly reference is The Arlington Institute (TAI), founded in 1989 by futurist John L. Petersen. It is a nonprofit research institute that specializes in thinking about global futures across a wide range of dimensions and creating conditions to influence rapid, positive change. It encourages systemic, non-linear approaches to planning and a belief that effective thinking about the future is enhanced by applying emerging technology. TAI strives to be an effective agent of advancement by creating intellectual frameworks and toolsets for understanding the transition in which we are living.

By understanding the trends, you can align your development plans with future trends. For example, if your industry is in flux over the next five years, your plan should prepare you to develop at a rate at least as fast as the industry and preferably much faster so you can lead rather than follow your industry change.

Tools and Exercises

Now that you have reviewed the tools and taken some or all of the assessments, it is time to synthesize what you have learned about yourself through a Strengths, Weaknesses, Opportunities, and Threats worksheet (SWOT) and through a series of reflection questions. For the SWOT analysis, please complete the worksheet below.

TABLE 4.1: SWOT ANALYSIS

Strengths *What sets you apart from most other people?*	**Opportunities** *What opportunities are open to those who have these strengths?*
Weaknesses *What do you need to improve?*	**Threats** *Do you have weaknesses that need to be addressed before you can move forward? Do any pose an immediate threat such as losing your job?*

Susan's Development Journey Continued

Susan will now walk through her worksheets and journal entries for analyzing her situation and strengths. Susan took the Enneagram assessment and tested primarily as a type six, loyalist with a backup style of achiever. Summary of type six: "I am a committed, security-oriented type. I am reliable, hard-working, responsible, and trustworthy. I am an excellent troubleshooter and can foresee problems and foster cooperation, but can also become defensive and anxious—running on stress while complaining about it. I can be cautious and indecisive. I can have problems with self-doubt."

She also took the MAP Developmental Perspective assessment. She scored at the strategist level of development, which puts her in the top five percent of all leaders on this scale. Strategist assessment on the MAP is comparable to "level 5 leader" referenced in Jim Collins' book *Good to Great*. We believe this is the level required to successfully implement successful change in large complex organizations. The strategist:

- perceives systematic patterns and long term trends
- makes sense of what they see rather than believing what they are told
- focuses on development, self-actualization, and authenticity
- lives their personal convictions according to internal standards
- tends toward a style of tenacity and humility—continually seeking creative paths to move toward vision
- relies on mutual interdependence with others
- is interested in personal development and helping others

SWOT WORKSHEET ANSWERS	
Strengths *What sets you apart from most other people?* ▪ Strong qualifications ▪ Diverse experience ▪ Ability to execute department's vision ▪ Able to work with people in a cooperative sense to accomplish a common goal ▪ Strong sense of urgency and drive for results ▪ Strong conviction to do the right thing ▪ Willing to accept feedback and strive to improve	**Opportunities** *What opportunities are open to those who have these strengths?* ▪ Deliver significant results ▪ Build overall capacity to sustain results ▪ Build a service that is well respected for academics and clinical outcomes ▪ Deliver thought leadership in prioritizing resource goals
Weaknesses *What do you need to improve?* ▪ Personally "untested" in the new chair role ▪ Current staffing requires change to fill open roles and address performance issues ▪ Divisions are not aligned with regard to purpose and departmental mission	**Threats** *Do you have weaknesses that need to be addressed before you can move forward? Do any pose an immediate threat?* ▪ Communication skills ▪ Perception as a new leader (able to respond to competing concerns effectively) ▪ Managing broad range of personalities of division leaders

Innovative Leadership Reflection Questions

To help you develop your action plan, it is time to further clarify your direction using reflection questions. The questions "What do I think/believe?" reflect your intentions. "What do I do?" questions reflect your actions. "What do we believe?" reflects the culture of your organization (i.e., work, school, community), and "How do we do this?" reflects systems and processes for your organization. This exercise is an opportunity to practice innovative leadership by considering your vision for yourself and how it will play out in the context of your life. You will define your intentions, actions, culture, and systems in a systematic manner.

Table 4.2 contains an exhaustive list of questions to appeal to a broad range of readers. Find a few that fit your own personal situation, and focus on the questions that seem the most relevant to you. We recommend that you answer one to three questions from each category.

TABLE 4.2: REFLECTION QUESTIONS
What do I think/believe? ▪ Given the direction the health care industry and world are unfolding, how do you believe you are positioned to be a leader in the future? ▪ Are you able to balance professional and personal commitments? How does your leadership style impact your ability to meet your overall life goals? ▪ How has your leadership style contributed to the organization's success? Have you done things that did not produce the results you had hoped? How would you change to produce different results? ▪ How would you like to impact the people who work for you? Have they grown and met their career goals while working for you? What have they contributed to the organization while working for you? ▪ If you are leading a change initiative, what will you need to change to lead this effort effectively? Will you lead the same way this time or will you change from what you have done in the past?
What do I do? ▪ How do you play to your strengths? ▪ How do you mitigate your weaknesses and threats? ▪ What opportunities do you want to take advantage of and what do you need to do to position yourself for success? ▪ How do you compensate for significant weaknesses? ▪ What assessments are you taking to gather objective data about your performance? This could include performance appraisals, developmental assessments, 360° feedback, or informal feedback from multiple sources. ▪ How do you communicate your personal changes and your sense of urgency to those around you who may be impacted by these changes?
What do we believe? ▪ Notice the various people and groups in your life (family, colleagues, boss, community, friends, etc.) and what they report as "urgent" right now. ▪ Anticipate how they will interpret your development and change. How will they talk about it? Specifically for your organization, how will the changes you aspire to make impact your constituents? ▪ Determine how your sense of urgency connects with the group's sense of urgency based on its priorities, goals, and pain points. ▪ How does the culture of your support system impact your beliefs about yourself and about leadership? Would these beliefs change if you changed who you spent time with? ▪ Based on developmental perspectives (if you have taken the MAP assessment), where is the cultural center of gravity in your support system? How are people with more open or broader perspectives perceived? How are people with earlier or smaller perspectives perceived? How will this impact your ability to change? (for more Information on developmental perspectives reference the Innovative Leadership Fieldbook) ▪ What are the cultural barriers to your changing? What are the cultural enablers? Will your changes be aligned with the organizational culture? Will they send a message that you do not value the culture?

How do we do this?

- What systems and processes are enablers and barriers that will impact my development?
- What processes and measures alert us to urgency in our system that we need to tend to? What are the early warning signs?
- What processes measure your progress? Are you progressing as measured by criteria that will increase your professional effectiveness? Are you progressing against your personal standards? How will your support system or organization reward or punish your changes based on the measures?
- Do the measures indicate a sense of urgency to you that support focusing on development?

Susan's Reflection Responses

We will now walk through Susan's answers from each section of Table 4.2. Simply follow along with Susan and answer her questions for yourself, or select questions that fit your current situation.

What do I think/believe?

- ***Given the direction the world is unfolding, how do you believe you are positioned to be a leader in the future?***

  Given the direction of academic medicine, I need to look at the department and determine the unique characteristics it brings. I believe we fill a niche of providing active translational research (bench to bedside) and highly sophisticated therapies that require complex inter-professional teams of highly skilled individuals. Among my key responsibilities are accomplishing operational efficiencies and demonstrating value in the field of medicine. Additionally, our department needs to teach the next generation of care providers.

  In this context, I believe I need to grow into my new role of department chair—to learn as much about the business of medicine as the science of medicine. I also need to further develop additional leadership skills. This includes learning to manage conflict and competing commitments.

- ***How has your leadership style contributed to the organization's success? Have you done things that did not produce the results you had hoped for? How would you change to produce different results?***

  I am a strong problem solver so I stay on top of issues often before they are visible to anyone else, and I create comprehensive solutions that align with the overall mission of the organization. As a higher level leader, I recognize that I need to empower others to identify and respond to issues, concerns, problems and challenges.

  I tend to be more hands on than this new role will require. By solving problems in advance of others getting involved, I take away the opportunity for them to learn and grow. This can, and has in cases, resulted in team members being overly dependent on my involvement.

I am committed to stepping back and allowing others to have the first opportunity to address issues and solve problems. I will still step in where necessary.

What do I do?

- ***How do you play to your strengths?***

  If you look at my SWOT analysis, you will see I focus on aligning all activities to meet the mission of the institution. I am able to fill a supportive mentoring role with junior faculty and staff. I also have very strong expertise in my own specialty field and am considered a thought leader and an expert in my area of research.

- ***How do you take advantage of opportunities?***

  Through a focus on leading a strong team. Our faculty and staff provide top quality education and serve our patients' needs by providing leading edge procedures. Additionally, we continue to build our funded research and publish our findings in high-impact academic journals.

- ***How do you communicate your personal changes and your sense of urgency to those around you who may be impacted by these changes?***

  I recognize that people look to me as their leader and that they take cues from my behavior as well as my demeanor. If they see me changing my behavior without understanding the cause, it could be unsettling to them—so I will share my personal development goals with those who might be most impacted. I believe this also positions me to model my values of ongoing learning and development. I want my team to understand my commitment to my own growth as well as theirs and this gives me an opportunity to demonstrate that commitment through my actions.

What do we believe?

- ***Anticipate how your change will be interpreted. How will colleagues talk about it? Specifically for your organization, how will the changes you aspire to make impact your constituents?***

  I believe change is uncomfortable for the person making the change. What my colleagues will likely experience is some inconsistency in my behavior. This is why letting them know my intention to change in advance will be important. I want to ensure that they interpret my learning new skills as the process of development rather than inconsistency or not delivering on my commitments. I have observed that people tend to think behavior changes happen quickly, when in reality developing new skills and habits happens gradually and is fraught with ups and downs. I believe the changes will have a positive overall impact on me, my constituents, and the organization, but they will take a number of months to be realized.

How do we do this?

- ***Which systems and processes are enablers and barriers that will impact my development?***

  We use a variety of personnel evaluation tools monitored through supervisory mid-year and annual review processes. We also use assessments (such as those referenced above). These provided me with great feedback and personal insight.

  Our appraisal process has been enlightening in identifying areas of opportunity and change. I say enlightening because it helped me see how my actions are perceived by others. Often as doctors, we do not get complete and honest feedback, and a good appraisal process goes a long way toward filling this information vacuum. I have had a very supportive boss who gave honest and helpful feedback—if not always what I wanted to hear.

  The biggest barrier I faced was the "get 'er done" mentality that limits our time to reflect and focus on performance improvement. While I love seeing results, it is easy to focus on results to the detriment of attention to the less urgent, but highly important, task of ongoing professional development.

- ***Which processes and measures alert us to urgency in our system that we need to tend to? What are the early warning signs?***

  Our early warning signs of problems include disenfranchised faculty or a high attrition rate. Additionally, warning signs are changes in the pace of productivity as measured by grant funding, clinical productivity, and publications. We could also see stagnation and lack of new initiatives rather than advancement and growth. On a more minor level, we could see a drop off in our referral base and lower metrics in our graduate medical education (GME) programs (not getting the best and brightest residents in our training programs).

- ***Your process of evaluating your situation and strengths***

  Now that you have followed Susan's responses, it is time to complete the worksheets. Based on your assessment results, if you have not done so already, complete the SWOT analysis in Table 4.1 and answer one to three questions from each section for yourself. By internalizing your strengths and opportunities, you can identify the gaps that, when filled, will help you to accomplish your vision. Understanding your weaknesses will also help you know what to avoid, what to improve, and what personal feedback to request from people skilled in those areas.

We encourage you to complete all of the exercises, taking your time and giving proper attention to gathering input from several different sources. When you have a clear picture of your strengths and opportunities, you will be ready to move to the next step. You may now find that you have a different or clearer perception about where you excel, and how those areas can complement your vision.

This chapter helped you clarify your strengths and weaknesses as a foundation for your personal transformation journey. Bear in mind that you are creating your own story through this process. The next chapter focuses on the framework for creating a development plan that will allow you to close the gap between your vision and where you are today.

Resources

Assessments

Enneagram for Leader Type: www.enneagraminstitute.com

Mature Adult Profile Assessment (MAP) and STAGES model for Developmental Perspectives: www.pacificintegral.com

The Leadership Circle 360° Assessment for Leadership Behaviors: www.theleadershipcircle.com

Resilience Assessment: www.metcalf-associates.com

Innovative Leadership Assessment: www.metcalf-associates.com

Susanne Cook-Greuter Research on Developmental Perspectives: www.cook-greuter.com

Book

Innovative Leadership Fieldbook. Metcalf and Palmer

What do I think/believe?

What do I do?

What do we believe?

How do we do this?

CHAPTER 5

Step 3: Plan Your Journey

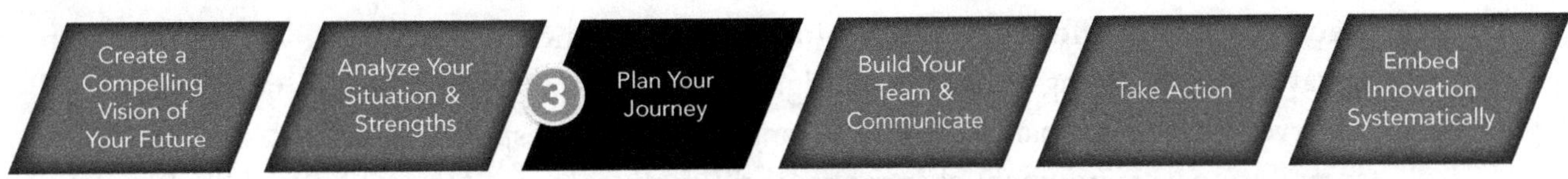

When you have a solid plan for your development journey, you begin investing your development time and energy based on your vision, your strengths and weaknesses, and your development goals. In order to stay motivated, it is important to experience a sense of measurable growth. Tangible results are especially crucial to implementing change, and demonstrating progress is a natural part of the expectation. An example is: If the dean wants me to show that I am a good leader before she will promote me, I need to show that I am "good" as measured by the dean's criteria. So, in this case, I would want to understand the criteria as well as know what she values, and build a plan that allows me to show those results. On the other hand, if I am developing for my own personal growth, I may not be as concerned about showing results to others, but will still want to feel I am making progress.

As you can imagine, some results will take longer than others to manifest. Our experience with clients has shown that leaders can certainly make quick progress in some areas, but progress in other areas may take years.

Your life situation will also impact your development. For example, a leader may be a great provider for his family, and this is a core value he holds. He might create meaningful results that help cultivate developmental growth by focusing on specific behaviors that will promote his well-being and success. In other words, through well-developed family relationships, he may simply experience a sense of progress ranging from a greater feeling of calm, clearer thinking, and better relationships with colleagues which will lead to better performance. He may also see measured results quantitatively using a 360° assessment (gaining feedback from several stakeholder groups at multiple levels within the organization including boss, peers, and subordinates) showing significant improvements in key leadership-related qualities. Another leader who wants to have a greater impact on the world may have an entirely different development focus and plan.

Consider the value of investing your energy in this journey as a way to foster meaningful change for the people closest to you. If you know, for example, that you have specific behaviors that are particularly difficult for your boss, an important colleague, or a loved one, you may want to prioritize those areas for improvement.

Options Development Plan Focus

To accomplish your vision, you may benefit from one or all of the following four developmental focuses:

- **Becoming more effective; developing new skills, and/or behaviors** – Changing behaviors and building skills that will significantly impact performance, as measured by observed behavioral change. As you advance in your job responsibilities and/or as the organizational environment changes, you will continually need to build new skills. These can range from an understanding of how to leverage a new electronic medical records system to keep people feeling engaged and connected to building a more effective medical practice. In this category, the focus is on skills that can be developed through training programs.

- **Building on your current strengths** – Development can take the form of focusing on enhancing current strengths. It can also focus on important behaviors that adversely impact success. Again, we recommend focusing 80 percent of your effort toward building on your strengths and passions and the other 20 percent toward shoring up your deficiencies. This is a general recommendation; it is important to remember that your specific situation and needs will be clear indicators of what changes are required for your continued growth and success.

- **Minimizing your weaknesses** – In the SWOT analysis, you may have identified some behaviors that impede further growth. These may have been behaviors that made you successful in your current development (sometimes referred to as overused strengths). Even so, part of your development is examining the events and behaviors that got you here and understanding which ones interfere with your success as defined by your vision. For example, you may identify yourself as someone who is on top of every task. As your responsibilities grow, you will delegate more, but you may still feel uncomfortable with your lack of knowledge of the details. Trying to manage the details to the level that made you successful will become a weakness as you move up. It is important to tend to these behavioral changes as part of your plan. The challenge here may be shifting the focus away from daily details toward strategic thinking and expanding your ability beyond one or a few core strengths to developing several additional capabilities.

As you begin building your capacity, you may want to consider two distinct, yet essential, areas—external capacity and internal capacity. Although the research emphasizing the importance of both is compelling, most of our formal training still focuses on hard skills (external capabilities). This exclusive emphasis leaves many leaders ill-prepared for, and in some cases uninformed about, the importance of internal capacity such as emotional intelligence and interpersonal skills. Research among Fortune 500 companies at Stanford University showed that 90 percent of those who failed as leaders did so because they lacked the interpersonal skills that are a critical component of emotional intelligence. This is confirmed by research conducted by the Center for Creative Leadership finding that poor interpersonal skills are a leading cause of derailment from executive-level positions. These terms are defined as:

- **External capacity (hard skills)** – Skills and behaviors associated with professional success. This is where most professional development efforts have been focused.
- **Internal capacity** – Includes intention, world view, purpose, vision, values, cultural norms, emotional stability, resilience, a sense of being grounded, overall personal well-being, intuition, balanced perspective, and attitude, and serves as the foundation for you to accomplish your deepest aspirations. Internal capacity is also required to move on to later stages of development.

In most organizations, the vast majority of development efforts focus on hard skills (including advanced degrees and certification programs), and thus, many leaders need to balance them by explicitly exercising internal capacity. To further describe this process, we use the term *mastery*, which simply means the capacity to not only produce results, but also to master the principles underlying those results. In other words, as a master, you can deliver results comfortably due to the internal capacity behind your skills and judgment.

Personal mastery involves enhancing your internal capacity to support the skills you have acquired while also removing barriers to your success. To help you achieve personal mastery, we recommend that you enrich your ongoing development plan and personal practices (activities we repeat until we master them, like our golf swing).

There are some important factors to consider when creating your plan. First, you will get more leverage if you cross-train or develop several areas at the same time. According to Ken Wilber (*AQAL Framework DVD*), there are benefits to cross-training beyond simply focusing on one area. For example, people who both lift weights and meditate tend to make greater improvements in both areas than those who do only one or the other. Evidence suggests that a combination of activities from different parts of our lives complement one another. This is quite true in the leadership arena as well.

A comprehensive plan will take into consideration each of the dimensions that are foundational to human experience: physical, emotional, mental, and spiritual (people not comfortable with the term *spiritual* can substitute *altruistic* or *purposeful*). If any of these elements is neglected, you are likely to find it will adversely impact your success in other areas over the long term.

Tools and Exercises

The range of tools is quite broad, so it is important to select something that feels safe and consistent with your values. The goal is to create a plan that you can follow and stick with to accomplish your goals. To help you get started, we put suggestions in Table 5.1. While several items fall within multiple categories, we attempted to classify them to be as mutually exclusive as possible. Some activities will provide benefits across several categories. An example of this is meditation, as it can help you manage your negative thinking, improve focus, balance emotions, and improve decision-making capacity.

Healthy development encompasses work in all areas. The practices you choose may evolve, and your practice may also fluctuate based on other life demands. We encourage you to maintain as much consistency as possible. Just as the benefit of exercise increases when you hit a specific frequency and duration, the same will be true for leadership development practices. The more you invest, the better your results will be.

TABLE 5.1: RECOMMENDATIONS FOR INTERNAL AND EXTERNAL CAPACITY BUILDING – ACTIVITIES TO CONSIDER INCORPORATING INTO PLAN

What activities can I do to impact my internal capacity (what I think and believe)?

- **Spiritual**
  - Define vision
  - Define values
  - Pray
  - Participate in religious practices
  - Participate in religious study
  - Seek spiritual counseling
  - Seek a spiritual teacher
  - Visualize goals
  - Become socially active: volunteer
- **Ethics**
  - Create guiding principles or values
  - Pay attention to ethics around you
  - Address situations you find unethical
  - Read and learn about ethics
- **Emotions (Emotional Quotient)**
  - Meditate
  - Seek therapy
  - Practice shadow exercises: the ability to find in yourself the things you find frustrating in others and address them as growth opportunities
  - Keep a journal
  - Seek coaching
  - Maintain strong friendships

What activities can I do to impact my external capacity?

- **Body**
  - Exercise
  - Yoga
  - Relaxation
  - Weight lifting
  - Mindful eating/healthy diet
  - Sufficient sleep
  - Cross-training
  - Reflection practices (do-reflect-learn)
- **Mind**
  - Read
  - Study
  - Attend lectures and discussion groups
  - Attend classes or workshops
  - Use perspective-taking exercises
  - Take stretch assignments
  - Volunteer for opportunities to build skills (charity work)
  - Manage polarities
  - Practice action inquiry
  - Practice Mindfulness-based stress reduction

What activities can I do that impact us as a group (what we think/believe)?

- Review the list of activities, and determine which can be completed in a group. What groups do I participate in, and do they have similar values?
- Develop a mission and values as a family. You may choose to set family meditation time or gym time to promote a family sense of focus and well-being. Many families share religious traditions and find that they provide a solid foundation and a shared set of values

What structures and/or groups will help? What groups or programs would support my development?

- Family activities could include how we eat, our exercise routines, our family reading time, our church or spiritual practice, and our volunteer activities
- Friend/social activities include what I do with my friends that support or hinder my development, such as exercise groups, emotional support, honest and accurate feedback, and dialogue practices
- Work events and support, including yoga classes, weight management support, fitness classes, insurance discounts for fitness, and smoking cessation programs
- Practice groups for development, such as Integral Transformative Practice, meditation, and church
- Study groups
- Formal education programs
- Informal education programs
- Fitness groups and programs, such as running clubs, ski clubs, exercise groups, and gym memberships

The following is a development plan template designed to help you create a plan that allows you to achieve your goals. This table focuses mainly on identifying opportunities and the intentions behind your desire to change.

TABLE 5.2: SKILL/BEHAVIOR DEVELOPMENT WORKSHEET
Evaluate and Select Skill/Behavioral Change Priorities – Worksheet

Key Actions	Detailed Action Planning	Behavior 1
Select behaviors	Which behaviors do I want to improve or change? Which behaviors do I perform well that I would like to enhance?	
What are the consequences of this behavior?	What will happen if I continue to demonstrate this behavior in the future? How will my service recipients be impacted? How will my career be impacted? How will my colleagues be impacted? How will my organization be impacted?	
Why do I demonstrate this behavior?	I have developed behaviors over the course of my life because they make sense. What has changed to make this behavior ineffective now?	
How would I like to perform in the future?	Write an end-result statement describing the changes I will make and the impact of those changes. What will an observer see when I have made these changes?	
Who will help me change?	Who could I ask to provide me with feedback on how I am doing? Who could be a good mentor?	
What type of support do I want?	Make an agreement with a person you trust about how you would like to support one another in changing behaviors. How will that person hold me accountable for taking this step? How will I support them in changing their behavior? Is there a group that will support me in the long term?	
What will I do or not do?	What other actions could I take? What am I willing to commit to doing? What am I committed to stopping?	
When will I complete actions?	When will I have completed action items?	

The next template was designed to synthesize development activities reflected in the prior worksheets.

We recommend that all goals be SMART, a term referenced in the November 1981 issue of *Management Review* by George T. Doran. Smart goals comprise five characteristics:

- **Specific** – Goals should be definitive and clearly defined. When goals are specific, it is clear to see when they are reached. To make goals specific, they must clarify exactly what is expected, why it is important, who's involved, where it is going to happen. *Overall example of a goal: Practice wants to improve the collection timeliness by 10% in one year as evidenced by collection reports.*

- **Measurable** – Establish concrete criteria for measuring progress toward the attainment of each goal you set. Measureable defines what and how much change we are expecting. *Example: 10 percent in one year is the measurement.*

- **Attainable** – When you identify goals that are most important to you, you begin to figure out ways you can make them come true. You develop the attitudes, abilities, skills, and financial capacity to reach them. You begin seeing previously overlooked opportunities to bring yourself closer to the achievement of your goals. "Attainable" ensures that our expectations are reasonable. *Example: One year and 10 percent are reasonable goals; 80 percent in one year is not an attainable goal.*

- **Realistic** – To be realistic, a goal must represent an objective toward which you are both willing and able to work. A goal can be both high and realistic. You are the only one who can decide the height of your goal, but be sure that every goal represents substantial progress. "Realistic" ensures that we have the capacity to meet our goal. *Example: 10 percent is also realistic. Our billing department can improve that amount in a year.*

- **Timely** – A goal should be grounded within an approximate time frame. Goals lacking time frames also lack urgency. Being timely ensures we have a deadline to meet our goals. As Dan Heath and Chip Heath state in *Switch: How to Change Things When Change is Hard:* "Some is not a number. Soon is not a time." *Example: One year is a defined period of time.*

Using the information from the worksheets and templates provided, you are now ready to complete your Development Planning Worksheet. This worksheet will serve as the foundation for the actions you will take to accomplish your goals, and should reflect your data gathering in the assessment chapter and your personal reflection.

TABLE 5.3: DEVELOPMENT PLANNING WORKSHEET Development Planning Worksheet				
Current State	Future State/Goal	Actions	By When?	Measure – How do you know?

Susan's Developmental Journey Continued

Susan will now walk through her worksheets and journal entries for planning her journey. When we last met Susan, she had completed analyzing her situation and strengths. Now she is evaluating the impact of one of a couple of her behaviors together to determine how to best address them through her development plan. The output of this exercise becomes direct input to her development plan.

Susan's Skill/Behavior Development Worksheet

EVALUATE AND SELECT SKILL/BEHAVIORAL CHANGE PRIORITIES

Key Actions	Detailed Action Planning	Behavior
Select behaviors	Which behaviors do I want to improve or change? Which behaviors do I perform well that I would like to enhance?	Very detail-oriented: need to move to higher level of focus
What are the consequences of this behavior?	What will happen if I continue to demonstrate this behavior in the future? How will my service recipients be impacted? How will my career be impacted? How will others be impacted?	1. Run the risk of "burn out" if time is not managed well 2. Risk disenfranchisement of the team by not trusting them with important matters
Why do I demonstrate this behavior?	I have developed behaviors over the course of my life because they make sense. What has changed to make this behavior ineffective now?	I am leading a larger group of individuals so I need to change to meet the new responsibilities.
How would I like to perform in the future?	Write an end-result statement describing the changes I will make and the impact of those changes. What will an observer see when I have made these changes?	I will step back from the details and empower division leaders to be creative and bring forth initiatives: managing with competence and support while simultaneously assuring that they are aligned with and supportive of my broader vision for the organization.
Who will help me change?	Who could I ask to provide me with feedback on how I am doing? Who could be a good mentor?	1. Health system leaders 2. Department administrator 3. Vice chairs
What type of support do I want?	Make an agreement with a person I trust about how I would like us to support one another in changing behaviors. How will that person hold me accountable for taking this step? How will I support them in changing their behavior?	I recognize that my stepping back will create a space and a mandate for my key reports to step forward. I expect us to provide mutual feedback on an ongoing basis about key initiatives as well as personal feedback about how the changes are going for them.
What will I do or not do?	What other actions could I take? What am I willing to commit to doing? What am I committed to stopping?	Have regular in-person meetings with key direct reports to listen to their ideas and initiatives as well gauge their level of comfort with the changes we are collectively making When differences of opinion arise I will promote dialogues. I will listen to their rationale and inquire before asserting my opinion.
When will I complete actions?	When will I have completed action items?	This will be an ongoing process of development and refinement and I expect to make significant progress in the first 6 months in my new role. Developing the leadership team will happen during the initial months, to be followed by a focus on mutual growth and development and continued refinement of our working relationship.

Now we will move from the evaluation of Susan's behavior to creating the development plan in which she determines what to do to address her behavior.

Susan's Development Plan

DEVELOPMENT PLANNING WORKSHEET

Current State	Future State/ Goal	Actions	By When?	Measure – How do you know?
Very detail-oriented	Develop skills to effectively administer larger more complex organization without getting bogged down in the details	Build trust in direct reports Enhance knowledge of operating a complex department Build emotional intelligence skills to monitor own preference to be heavily detail oriented Build competencies: technical knowledge and emotional intelligence	Begin immediately and make significant progress in 6 months.	Feedback from others on effectiveness: dean peers subordinates
New in current role	Develop skills to be recognized as highly effective and efficient Department leader	Develop understanding of organizational structure of the department and interconnections with other elements of the organization including budgeting, HR, operations Build self-awareness and professional presence Enhance ability to work effectively with (including manage) broad spectrum of individuals	Begin immediately. and make significant progress in 6 months	Feedback from others on effectiveness: dean peers subordinates

DEVELOPMENT PLANNING WORKSHEET

		Enhance skills in analyzing, problem-solving and decision-making, and building buy-in fo decisions by attending a workshop. Build skills and relationships to enhance interactions with other departments, the broader university structure, and outside entities Build competencies: technical knowledge; emotional intelligence; problem-solving prowess and decision-making; knowledge of health care; effective communication		
Current staffing requires change to fill open roles and address performance issues	Develop skills that will facilitate the team building in the department	Understand personality types and individual ability to deal with complexity and professional relationships with each employee Consider team-building session(s) Structure departmental roles and responsibilities clearly and hold people accountable Build competencies: Effective communication; emotional intelligence; skill of facilitation	Solid skill development in first 90 days in role and continue to build	Feedback from team
Divisions are not aligned with regard to purpose and mission	Functioning as "one department" focusing on meeting the mission rather than competing with one another	Address team measures and conflicting measures: align systems Conduct team-building sessions to build culture that sees us as "one department" not separate and competing divisions Build competencies: effective communication; emotional intelligence; skill of facilitation	Solid progress in my first 90 days in role and continue to build	Feedback from division leaders; culture change at department meetings

Innovative Leadership Reflection Questions

To help you develop your action plan, it is time to further clarify your direction using reflection questions. The questions for "What do I think/believe?" reflect your intentions. "What do I do?" questions reflect your actions. The questions "What do we believe?" reflect the culture of your organization (i.e., work, school, community), and "How do we do this?" questions reflect systems and processes for your organization. This exercise is an opportunity to practice Innovative Leadership by considering your vision for yourself and how it will play out in the context of your life. You will define your intentions, actions, culture, and systems in a systematic manner.

Table 5.4 contains an exhaustive list of questions to appeal to a broad range of readers. You will likely find that a few of these best fit your own personal situation. Focus on the questions that seem the most relevant. We recommend you answer one to three questions from each of the categories.

TABLE 5.4: QUESTIONS TO GUIDE THE LEADER AND ORGANIZATION
What do I think/believe? ▪ What are my priorities for development? Are they reflected in the plan I created? ▪ Am I willing to make the changes necessary to meet my goals? ▪ What do I consider personal short-term wins? ▪ Which wins do I want to see in what time frame? Is this reasonable? ▪ What do I consider a win for my team? ▪ What do I consider a win for the organization? ▪ Which short-term wins will be really important to key people in my life? ▪ How do I stay motivated to work toward goals that will take a long time, or a lifetime, to accomplish? How will I think about life changes? ▪ Have I taken into account the whole range of activities I need to create a sustainable change, such as involving others and creating a plan that I can live with long-term?
What do I do? ▪ How do I translate my vision into long- and short-term goals? ▪ Are my goals SMART? ▪ What are my financial goals and milestones? ▪ Is this a plan that is sustainable in the long-term? Will accomplishing my short-term wins motivate me to stay on track with my long-term plan? ▪ Does my plan contain the foundation work as well as skill-building (i.e., personal health as well as leadership competencies)? ▪ Which wins can I identify and support that solve problems and are seeds for future shifts? ▪ Which changes in my behavior will demonstrate a strong statement to others and encourage their ongoing support, while possibly modeling changes that could also serve others?

What do we believe?
▪ Which wins will provide meaningful tangible and emotional results, and gain support from key stakeholders in my life? ▪ Which wins will encourage others to engage in their own personal/professional growth initiatives? ▪ Which stories can we tell others about the wins that were shared with the organization to encourage them to focus on their development? ▪ Which wins are reinforced by our culture and values? Which wins would be opposed to our culture and values?
How do we do this?
▪ How do I align my goals and short-term wins with the organization such that I receive support for the changes I am making? How do I ensure that early wins are important to key stakeholders? ▪ How do I track and measure my wins and their impact against overall personal and organizational goals? Do I have early warning signals or measures? ▪ Are my wins aligned with the larger organizational objectives? ▪ Does the organization reinforce and reward the behavioral changes I am making? ▪ How will I connect my personal wins to the organizational vision and measures to demonstrate the impact of my small steps forward?

Susan's Reflection Responses

We will now walk through Susan's answers to one or two questions from each section of Table 5.4. Simply follow along with Susan to answer the questions for yourself or select the questions that fit your current situation.

What do I think/believe?

- ***What do I consider personal short-term wins?***

  My biggest short-term wins include building my management team and stepping back from the details (see behavior change priority worksheet). This means I need to change my own behavior by stepping back from details and work closely with my team to ensure that they are stepping in. Since I am new in this role, I am not completely sure how much this will go. I think my predecessor had behaviors similar to mine—being heavily involved—which is why I have these behaviors now. This means that when I step back the team will need to make a change from how they worked with my predecessor. Getting feedback from the team will let me know if I am on track.

- ***What do I consider a win for my team?***

  Growing strong leaders is a big win for all involved. I want department leaders to work together as a cohesive team. I have always preferred to build a strong team of people—any of whom could step into my role. While I have worked hard to earn this role, I aspire to continue to grow in my career, and for that to happen. I need to grow the leadership team. Additionally, my values tell me that I need to help others grow, which is why I joined academic medicine. If I were to focus on growing faculty without growing students and residents, I would be out of alignment. So, to sum this up, growing my team is a win for me and for the team as well as for the overall training program.

What do I do?

- ***Are my goals SMART?***

My goals are SMART enough to guide my development. As I look at my development plan, I assigned timeframes to the goals in the plan so they are indeed time bound. They are specific in that they connect back to competencies in chapter two that provide clear details. They are attainable in that I believe I can accomplish them, and realistic in the timelines I set. I believe they can be measured using assessment tools, observation and feedback, but they are not as clearly defined as some less complex personal goals (such as engaging in exercise five times per week).

Is this a plan that is sustainable in the long-term? Will accomplishing my short-term wins motivate me to stay on track with my long-term plan?

I believe this is sustainable as the team and I grow together, and we will all see benefits from the changes. Success breeds success, so short-term wins will give me and team members' confidence, which will build momentum and reinforce our commitment to the plan. I have seen in the short time since taking on this role that others want to grow and learn. I believe we will build on our successes. Doctors are goal oriented and this team is no exception. We will take our wins and go on to the next goal.

What do we believe?

- ***Which wins will encourage others to engage in their own personal/professional growth initiatives?***

As I have stated before, I think team success will breed the desire for greater success. Fear of failure and pride in accomplishment are great motivators, and I think our experienced and motivated team understands that our personal and professional successes depend on each other and the team's success. Everyone—for personal pride and job security—wants to be recognized for their input and achievements. It is always what we have or can accomplish together. New, inexperienced team members might take some time to mature into understanding this, but if surrounded by good mentors, most will get to this point and those who do not may not belong on the team.

- ***Which stories can we tell others about the wins that were shared with the organization to encourage them to focus on their development?***

Our department has had many wins;we continue to win grant funding, and our research is being published in high-impact journals. By making the changes I am shooting for, I believe I can support the overall department and its faculty and staff in meeting its goals. We continue to celebrate each win in funding and publications as a group success. We have had many recently, and each one seems to build on the prior. This continued success will rely on our ability to pull together as one department. As momentum builds, so do the expectations, and in fact, we risk falling short of our goals because of our own success.

How do we do this?

- ***Are my wins aligned with the larger organizational objectives?***

  The organization has a set of goals and objectives as outlined by senior management and all plans cascade from top down to support the overall target. With this said, I believe the team's wins in research, in developing highly sophisticated therapies that require complex inter-professional teams of highly skilled individuals, as well as teaching the next generation of care providers, are fully aligned with the institution.

- ***Does the organization reinforce and reward the behavioral changes I am making?***

  Yes, the organization is supportive and has encouraged me to get a coach to help me move into the new leadership role. They have continued to reward my growth as is evident by this promotion. They promote a culture of respect for physicians building strong leadership skills. They understand that in this ever more complex time, our leaders are not only practicing but also transforming the way we deliver medical care and building the teams and infrastructure to do so. This is a much different expectation than that of our predecessors just ten years ago.

Your Process of Creating Your Development Plan

Now that you have followed Susan's descriptions, it is time to complete the worksheets. Based on your assessment results, if you have not done so already, complete the SWOT analysis in Table 4.1 and answer one to three questions from each section in Table 4.2 for yourself. By internalizing your strengths, as well as opportunities, you can identify the gaps that, when filled, will help you accomplish your vision. Additionally, understanding your weaknesses will help you know what to avoid, what to improve, and what personal feedback to request from people skilled in those areas.

This chapter provided you with the tools and templates to create your development plan, and will help to close the gap between where you are today and compared with your vision of where you are today and where you want to be . The plan will greatly enhance your efforts toward actualizing where you want to be, as well as making a positive impact on the world. Keep in mind that it is easy to create a plan that is too ambitious or complex. We encourage you to commit to small changes you can complete and then update your plan after you have accomplished your initial goals. The next chapter focuses on selecting the guiding team that will help you implement your plan.

Resources

Books

Path of Least Resistance, Learning to Become the Creative Force in Your Own Life. Tool: Structural Tension. Robert Fritz.

Action Inquiry, The Secret of Timely and Transforming Leadership. Bill Torbert and Associates.

Crucial Conversations, Tools for Talking when Stakes are High. Patterson, Grenny, McMillan, Switzler.

Fifth Discipline Fieldbook, Strategies and Tools for Building a Learning Organization. Art Kleiner, Peter Senge, Richard Ross, Bryan Smith, Charlotte Roberts.

The Life We Were Given, A Long Term Program for Realizing Potential of Body, Mind, Heart and Soul. George Leonard and Michael Murphy.

Polarity Management: Identifying and Managing Unsolvable Problems. Barry Johnson

DVD

Integral Life Practice Starter Kit. Integral Institute (3-2-1 Shadow Workshop and Big Mind).

CD Set

Mindfulness in Motion – A Daily Low Dose Mindfulness Practice. Maryanna Klatt, PhD

Online resource and tools

HeartMath™ meditation practices and emWave to monitor heart activity. www.heartmath.org.

What do I think/believe?

What do I do?

What do we believe?

How do we do this?

CHAPTER 6

Step 4: Build Your Team and Communicate

You are working on the fourth step in the process: Build Your Team & Communicate.

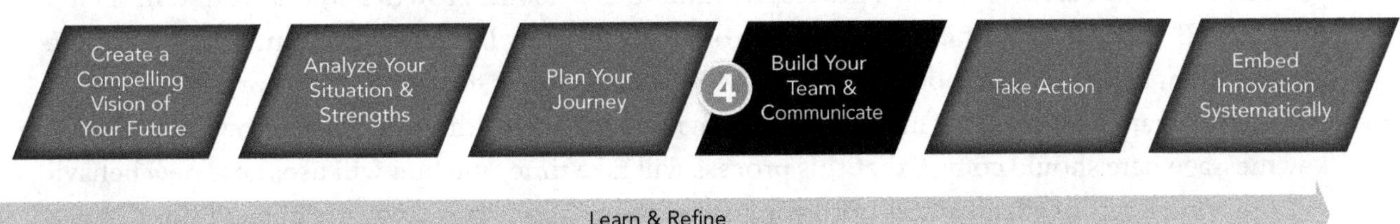

In this chapter, you will begin to identify the individuals you want to support your personal and professional development, and the specific roles you envision them playing during this transition. After selecting these people, you will consider the best ways to communicate your needs and receive their feedback. Here, you will carefully choose individuals you feel will be most supportive of your growth. Consider who is involved in your development and who is not. Your selection criteria should include: experience and skills in areas you want to develop, a high level of unconditional personal support, ability to offer constructive and valuable feedback, capacity to support your transformation, and ability to offer professional support and advocacy.

You will benefit from choosing a diverse yet trusted set of people to support your development. This is particularly beneficial if you plan to make changes that will significantly impact them as well. These people can come from various areas of your life, both personal and professional, and can have differing levels of involvement. Some, for example, could be fairly casual, such as a colleague who is willing to give you feedback after a meeting about a specific behavior you may be experimenting with to meet a goal of improved interpersonal skills. At the other end of the spectrum, you could engage in a more methodical, long-term agreement with a formal mentor or coach. You will also want to consider the role your spouse or partner plays if you are in a relationship. Anyone involved must agree to give you honest and supportive feedback. The common thread for the people you ultimately invite to share in your journey is a firm trust and belief that, above all else, their support is unquestionably in the interest and service of your growth and success.

As another option, your development support could be found within a team setting. For example, if your goal is to run a marathon, your development support could come from a range of sources. It could be as simple as joining a running group to support a fitness goal. You might recruit specific individual running partners. Other options could include finding expertise from third-party sources like running magazines or online groups that discuss tips and progress. You may even select a group with the explicit purpose to strongly hold each other more accountable.

Professional development can be supported in similar ways. You have a broad range of choices when looking for support. Organizations range from coaching and training firms to companies that help you improve your presentation skills. Depending on your needs, your individual selection of development support may have components of some or all of these choices. Some may be focused on hard skills, while others, like a coach, take on a more generally supportive role.

After you have selected your support team, the next step will be deciding on methods for each person to communicate authentic feedback. This is the stage in which you ask others for specific kinds of support, including possible behavioral changes on their part. You will be letting people around you know that you are engaged in a process of ambitious personal growth and that you want their feedback. Because people often create a sense of personal safety by being able to predict how others around them behave, it is important to inform the people closest to you that you are taking on a structured change process that may involve behaviors with which they are likely to be unfamiliar. The key message here should convey that this process will take time, and you will use these new behaviors with varying levels of effectiveness until you master them. You may say you are changing and may act inconsistently for some period of time while you master new skills.

While the information you share will change over time, the need for communication is critical throughout your development process. Communication will happen with different groups of people at various times, and will likely take on different tones depending on the audience and degree of impact. Some people will simply need to understand that overall change is underway, while you may want others to make significant contributions to support your behavioral change. What you communicate and when will depend on your relationship with the individual or group, and the type of support you are asking for.

As mentioned earlier, during your process, you may also be asking others to change. For example, in the workplace, you may be communicating information beyond just the scope of work in order to help your staff, coworkers, associates, employees, and direct reports develop stronger technical knowledge. Moreover, you may want others to change their overall style of communication with you. As you model these new behaviors, be aware that some of your colleagues will adapt quite naturally, while others will require more specific and formal discussions to adjust to this new way of relating. As another example, you may want to delegate more and possibly different tasks, as well as give people more freedom to determine how they accomplish assigned tasks. In this case, you could open a dialogue explaining that you are trusting them to determine the most effective approach and will be available to offer support if additional input is needed. Though many individuals would respond favorably to the openness, some will likely be confused if you are not explicit with what you are trying to accomplish.

Support Team Selection Criteria

Providing support to someone who is committed to a process of personal growth is an honor and a tremendous responsibility. It is important to select a support team judiciously since you are requesting these individuals be trusted advisors.

The following is a rough list of key selection factors as a starting point for you to consider when selecting your team. You may find other factors that are also important to you.

Performance: Consider selecting people who have mastered concepts, skills, or behaviors that you would like to develop in yourself. Performance could be as simple as that person having expertise in your field or a field you want to explore. He or she could have strong interpersonal skills and empathy, or have hard skills such as financial analysis that you would like to enhance in yourself. These individuals could also be people you respect in general. If you are focused on developing advanced leadership skills, you could certainly benefit from the mentoring and support of someone you believe is successful against these measures.

Coaching: Consider having a person who is paid as an independent expert in the process of development and/or therapy. Most have undergone rigorous training or have significant experience in the field to support your development and success. As they are independent, they are generally free of the natural bias held by family members, friends, and colleagues. Working with the right coach can be very valuable, significantly accelerate the development process, and help you overcome barriers.

Therapy: Having someone who is an experienced psychotherapist can be very beneficial. A good therapist, who is a good fit with your style and needs, can help you make changes much more quickly and efficiently than if you try to work through issues yourself.

Personal or Family Connection: People from your family supporting your development could include siblings, a partner or a spouse, or a close friend who feels like family. Ideally, they will help you maintain a balanced perspective of your life as a whole based on a historical connection, rather than just the immediate view of a new coach or therapist. They will also help you think through the impact of your changes on your family system. It is important to balance your development and professional focus with your family commitments.

Willingness and ability to commit time to your development: This is imperative. Ask those who are committed to supporting your development how to optimize your time together and also allot time to discuss your mutual needs. The idea is that everyone should benefit from a clear understanding of how to both support the growth process and create healthy reciprocity. It will also be important to consider the time commitment you desire. Be willing to explore options that allow you to minimize the amount of time you request. You may consider creative options like volunteering for a board that your mentor or support person is on. This would allow you to learn directly and also support that person in meeting their objectives.

Consider not only who to select, but also who to avoid. Keep in mind that there are many very well-meaning people who would love to help, but, realistically, who are overcommitted and cannot provide the type of support you seek. Others may lack strong support skills, like the ability to give open and honest feedback. If someone lacks the time or skills to provide helpful advice, delivered in a supportive way, you should not include them. What you do not need during an intense development process is to waste time and energy with someone whose involvement could derail you.

Tools

The following worksheets are designed to help you connect your development action plan with the people who will help you accomplish these goals. They will fulfill different roles, ranging from encouragement and support to providing skilled expertise. You might also choose to include those who may be more directly impacted by the changes you are making. The more information you can provide during the process, the more likely they will be to support you or communicate their concerns to help you accomplish your goals. For an example, see Susan's answers following each worksheet.

TABLE 6.1: SUPPORT TEAM WORKSHEET
Support Team Worksheet

Goal	Type of Support I Need	Role	Skills/ Knowledge or Other Criteria	Arrangement

Susan's Worksheet

When we last connected with Susan, she had created his development plan. She is now evaluating who will help her implement her goals.

SUPPORT TEAM WORKSHEET

Goal	Type of Support I Need	Role	Skills/ Knowledge or Other Criteria	Arrangement
Develop skills to effectively administer larger more complex organization without getting bogged down in the details	Coach Trusted colleagues Attend classes	Tools to reframe thinking about best use of talent to accomplish all goals Provide feedback on behaviors	Competency of technical knowledge Competency of emotional intelligence	Coaching bi-weekly As needed from colleagues
Develop skills to be recognized as efficient and effective department leader	Coach Trusted colleagues/ employees Dean or chief medical officer (boss) Attend professional development workshops Read journals/ professional literature	Provide tools and frameworks for effective leadership Feedback delivered by assessments Provide feedback on behaviors	Competency: technical knowledge Competency: emotional intelligence Competency: Problem-solving prowess and decision-making Competency: Knowledge of health care Competency: Effective communication	Coaching bi-weekly As needed from colleagues and dean
Develop skills that will facilitate the team building in the department	Coach Attend professional development workshops Read literature	Learn team effectiveness skills Practice skills with existing team Provide input on individual and team accountabilities	Competency: Effective communication Competency: emotional intelligence Facilitation	Monthly
Functioning as "one department" focusing on meeting the mission rather than competing with one another	Other chair colleagues Department vice chairs	Share strategies that promote collaboration and culture of cohesion	Competency: Effective communication Competency: emotional intelligence Facilitation	Quarterly and periodic as needed

Once you determine your support team and their corresponding roles, you will want to figure out communication, timing, and expectations. This is the place to consider the kind of feedback you might expect from others to ensure you are making meaningful progress. This communication can provide you with invaluable information and feedback that is critical for your success. Since your plan is based on your own intuitive senses, the ongoing data should confirm your assumptions and serve as a feedback mechanism to refine your thinking.

TABLE 6.2: COMMUNICATION PLAN WORKSHEET
Communication Planning Worksheet

Who	What to Communicate	What They Can Expect From You	What You Want From Them	How Often

The following table is from Susan's Communication Worksheet. You can use it as an example of how one may use communication when managing change both personally and within an organization.

COMMUNICATION PLANNING WORKSHEET				
Who	**What to Communicate**	**What They Can Expect From You**	**What You Want From Them**	**How Often**
Coach	Clearly stated goals and objectives Progress Challenges Reflections of ongoing activities	Clear communication Commitment to development Doing the activities required to meet goals and objectives	Listen Advise Engage and interact Provide honest feedback	Bi-weekly
Trusted colleagues/ employees	Clearly stated goals and objectives Specific behavior changes and feedback you are seeking	Try new behaviors and seek feedback Listen to advice and feedback Continue to try new behaviors	Listen Advise Engage and interact Provide honest feedback	Ongoing as needed
Dean or Chief Medical officer (boss)	Clearly stated goals and objectives Challenges and successes	High performance	Motivation Engagement Ongoing skill- building	Monthly
Other chair colleagues Department vice chairs	Clearly stated goals and objectives about acting as one division	Aligning the divisions to work as one highly effective department with common purpose and synergies Honest assessment of current state Open communications Objective analysis of current and changing state	Provide examples of how they have solved similar issues Listen and analyze Direct and honest feedback	Monthly

Innovative Leadership Reflection Questions

To help you develop your action plan, it is time to further clarify your direction using reflection questions. The questions for "What do I think/believe?" reflect your intentions. "What do I do?" questions reflect your actions. The questions "What do we believe?" reflect the culture of your organization (i.e., work, school, community), and "How do we do this?" questions reflect systems and processes for your organization. This exercise is an opportunity to practice Innovative Leadership by considering your vision for yourself and how it will play out in the context of your life. You will define your intentions, actions, culture, and systems in a systematic manner.

Table 6.3 contains an exhaustive list of questions to appeal to a broad range of readers. A few will likely fit your own personal situation; focus on the ones that seem the most relevant. We recommend you answer one to three questions from each of the categories.

TABLE 6.3: QUESTIONS TO GUIDE THE LEADER AND ORGANIZATION
What do I think/believe? ▪ What qualities do I want in the people I ask to support my personal change? ▪ What qualities will I eliminate from my current and future team? ▪ How do I think my change will impact those close to me? ▪ Will my change help those close to me become more successful according to their definition of success? ▪ Why would others spend their time and energy to help me develop? ▪ How much support do I expect from others? ▪ Am I making reasonable requests of those close to me? ▪ Am I looking for others in the medical arenas who are making similar changes? ▪ Do I want people around me to change along with me? ▪ Do I need to improve my communication skills to improve my ability to seek support for my growth? ▪ Because my development may be a very personal and even private choice, what am I willing to communicate to others? ▪ How do I think my preference for privacy or sharing will impact others' responses to my changes and their ability to do what they need to do to either support me or accomplish their jobs? Do I solicit their input and support? If so, how and when? ▪ What personal stories (actions and emotions) will convey my commitment to my personal change in a heartfelt manner while also empowering others to act? ▪ Do I need to communicate anything to the organization or only to my support group?

What do I do?

- Who do I ask to participate in my change?
- How do I determine and communicate the criteria for the right people to support me? "Right" includes personality traits, innate capabilities, skills, knowledge, time, and willingness
- Once I know the criteria, who are the right people and how do I figure out what roles I would like them to take to support my continued success? How do I invite them to support this important personal transformation?
- Who do I need to support my development for it to be successful? How can my personal development activities or successes help these key people meet their personal objectives?
- Who may become a barrier to my change? How do I mitigate their negative impact? What are immediate steps and longer-term actions?
- What commitments and actions should I take that demonstrate my belief that change is possible?
- How do I "walk the talk" and show my conviction through my actions? Am I making the changes I say I will? Am I asking for input and acting on the recommendations others give me? If I do not take their recommendations, do I explain why?
- How do I ask for feedback? Am I clear about what information would be helpful to me and what information would not be helpful?
- How do I convey my request for input and support when I fall short of my stated goals at points along the way?
- How do I deliver messages tailored to different supporters that motivate them to continue to help me accomplish my goals?
- Can I be a role model for others during my change process to encourage them to expand their own capabilities?
- How do I convey messages that will make strong statements using the languages of both feelings and logic to appeal to each individual supporter?
- How do I demonstrate humility and genuine appreciation of the support others are providing?
- How do I communicate progress along with new challenges and my commitment to what I am doing?
- How do I communicate the facts and my hopes for the future?
- How do I communicate that the balance between challenge and overload is important, and that I want to maintain balance as I move toward meeting my personal vision?
- How do I communicate my need and desire for accurate feedback?
- What do I communicate when my situation and priorities change?

What do we believe?

- What are the social and cultural norms that dictate the type of support I should ask for and expect?
- How do we use my personal change as an opportunity to test new behaviors and demonstrate their positive impact on the group (professional organization, family, community)?
- Do the current social and cultural norms still fit for where I am/we are going?
- Do I have the right support to change the culture of our group to allow me to sustain the changes I am trying to make?
- What are our beliefs about who does the communicating? How much information do they share? How often? Do we solicit input or just convey information?
- What is the appropriate language and message content based on the values, goals, language, and culture of each audience segment (physicians, staff)?
- What type of feedback will I seek from supporters to determine if they are supportive of my personal changes? This may be objective or subjective
- Does our current organizational culture and approach to communicating support me in making the changes I am trying to make?

How do we do this?

- What are the key skills and behaviors that support my transformation and are necessary to my team? What are the gaps between my current support team and the team needed to support transformation? Do I have the right people available with the right skills and behaviors? Do I need to augment my support team with professionals such as a coach, therapist, spiritual advisor, clergy, colleague, or boss?
- What is the best combination of approaches for me to meet my support needs? Does this include hiring a coach, or scheduling regular lunches with a trusted colleague?
- What trust-building activities can we conduct to improve my degree of comfort with those supporting me?
- What personal and professional metrics should I track to understand if I am seeking and receiving the appropriate level of support?
- If the transformation is a long one, how do I acknowledge the support others are providing? What happens if someone I thought would be a good supporter does not work out?
- Am I communicating what supporters believe is important to them? Do they see the progress they hope to see?
- How do I communicate wins to stakeholders to sustain their reinforcement and energy?
- What is my communication approach and plan? Who wants information? When? Through what medium? What are the key messages? How do I keep multiple supporters informed with the right amount of information at the right time to enhance buy-in and support for my behavioral change?
- What is my communication? Do we have any applicable stories or narratives? ("Remember the time xxx did xxx? Guess what happened to me this week.")?
- Can we combine and/or eliminate any current communications? Are we talking about things that are not supportive of the change I want to make?
- Would communication be more effective if my changes were discussed in conjunction with other topics that either impact or are impacted by my change? If, as a group, we are trying to change, maybe we can talk about our progress, or about personal and organizational changes and how they are linked and impact one another.

Susan's Response to Reflection Questions

We will now walk through Susan's answers to one or two questions from each section of Table 6.3. Simply follow along with Susan to answer the questions for yourself, or select the questions that fit your current situation.

What do I think/believe?

- ***How do I think my change will impact those close to me?***

  I hope it will allow me to be a more engaged leader who listens more and tells less. The people I work closely with are very experienced and have had considerable opportunities to engage with me in many different situations. Because of this, they will benefit from a more open and dynamic style that gives them more autonomy and opportunity.

- ***Why would others spend their time and energy to help me develop?***

  I believe we are all connected so they will benefit from my growth and may very well grow themselves at the same time. High functioning leaders are easier to work with; they bring more creativity and freedom. They (my team) will feel less constrained when working with me allowing them to be more empowered and creative.

What do I do?

- ***What commitments and actions should I take that demonstrate my belief that change is possible?***

  I will articulate my planned changes to my close colleagues and solicit their feedback on my progress as well as asking for their recommendations to further my ability to meet my stated goals. My goals should be clear and measurable so that I can hold myself accountable.

- ***Can I be a role model for others during my change process to encourage them to expand their own capabilities?***

  Yes, by embracing my own development and leading by example I will serve as a role model for those working for me. This will be accentuated because I plan to share my development goals and seek their input. This should inspire others and create an environment of continual learning and growth.

What do we believe?

- ***Do I have the right support to change the culture of our department to allow me to sustain the changes I am trying to make?***

  I believe the answer is yes. I already have the support of the majority of division directors and all see the necessity for leadership and organizational change in response to the changing health care environment. I plan to explain why I want to change and demonstrate positive success to build on what they are already doing well.

- ***Do the current social and cultural norms still fit for where I am/we are going?***

  The norms are fluid and changing as we move more through dramatic changes in the health care environment. We need to adapt to shrinking research dollars, a shift from productivity to results oriented health care and a call for greater accountability and transparency. While I cannot control these forces, I can manage how we respond and the culture shift required for success.

How do we do this?

- ***What is the best combination of approaches for me to meet my support needs? Does this include hiring a coach or scheduling regular lunches with a trusted colleague?***

  A combination of support is necessary. I have a supportive family to help me retain my resilience. I have a trusted support group of close professional colleagues who serve as a sounding board and provide honest feedback. I work for an organization that is willing to fund coaching and leadership development programs. I also have resources within my professional organizations and boards that will provide an external perspective.

- ***What is my communication? Do we have any applicable stories or narratives? ("Remember the time xxx did xxx? Guess what happened to me this week.")***

  The CEO recently spoke at a conference about the improvements within the health system attributed to a cohesive program of leadership development. He provided statistics as well as sample case studies of successes. He also spoke directly about his personal journey. Many other leaders are willing to share their personal stories including their mistakes, obstacles, challenges and ultimately successes.

- ***Your Individual Process to Build Your Team and Communicate***

  Now that you have seen the worksheets and read through Susan's narratives, it is time to complete the worksheets and answer the questions for yourself. Based on your support preferences, complete Table 6.1 (Support Team worksheet) and Table 6.2 (Communication Planning worksheet), then answer one to three questions from each section in Table 6.3.

This chapter serves to help you clarify your supporters and communication plan as you begin defining your feedback sources. This is the plan that will provide you with expertise, emotional support, buy-in, and feedback for your development. While creating a communication plan may seem extraneous, never underestimate the value of both emotional/moral support and communication with those who will be affected by your changes. This could be as simple as talking to your spouse or family about the way changing your routine may impact them, while letting them know you appreciate their willingness to be flexible.

Resources

Books

Crucial Conversations, Tools for Talking when Stakes are High. Patterson, Grenny, McMillan, Switzler.

Fifth Discipline Fieldbook, Strategies and Tools for Building a Learning Organization. Art Kleiner, Peter Senge, Richard Ross, Bryan Smith, Charlotte Roberts. See section on Conversational Recipes.

The Fifth Discipline: Strategies and Tools for Building a Learning Organization. Senge, Kleiner, Roberts, Smith

What do I think/believe?

What do I do?

What do we believe?

How do we do this?

CHAPTER 7

Step 5: Take Action

You are working on the fifth step in the process: Take Action.

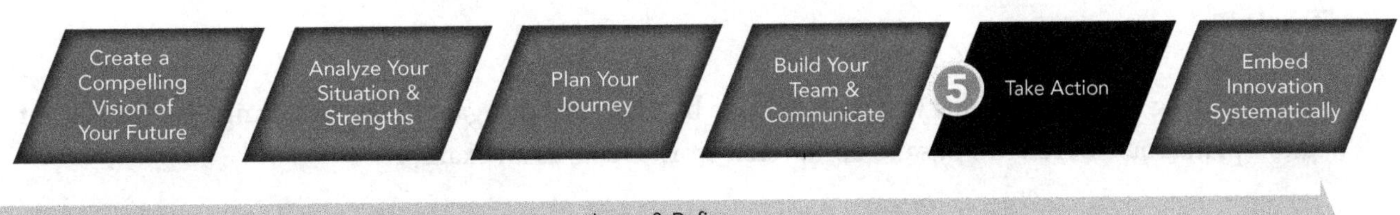

Now that you have created a plan to become an innovative leader and have defined your support team, it is time to take action. Your plan should spell out which actions you want to take, how often, and who can support your progress.

As you begin realizing your vision, you may start to identify challenges to your growth and development. Barriers are simply a normal part of any transformative process; we have provided a number of useful tools to help pinpoint and navigate them successfully.

An important part of your success is the belief that you can make progress and sustain growth in your leadership ability. You've already developed a strong foundation by creating a compelling vision and analyzing unique challenges and opportunities to determine what actions you needed to take to achieve your goals.

Be aware that this stage can take tremendous focus and energy. Many people stumble here, especially when the change process becomes difficult and the demands of balancing life requirements take on greater urgency. Think, for example, of how many times you may have joined a gym, but did not follow your plan to go there as frequently as you'd intended. Implementing your plan requires a deep commitment to your growth and also an understanding of the barriers you will face based on your personality type or history with implementing change. As barriers surface, you have the ability to remove them or modify your course with the support of your team.

With this in mind, allow yourself some flexibility in your development process instead of viewing your plan as fixed. See your plan as an initial starting point, or a working hypothesis about how you will develop. With that perspective, you can better use the challenges you face as a way to provide feedback on your original hypothesis and modify it as you go along. In other words, rather than viewing these obstacles as threats, you have the opportunity to naturally incorporate them as fine-tuning mechanisms. For each challenge you face, carefully consider the unique learning opportunity and how to use it to help you implement your plan. Since personal development is a long-term journey, you will have many opportunities to face these challenges and take corrective actions.

Lastly, your support team will play a meaningful role in helping make the plan sustainable. They will offer you input and feedback as well as encouragement during times when you struggle. Even though you specifically chose the changes and goals within your plan, it is often still helpful to have a built-in system of accountability. When you run into inner resistance and difficulty, connect with someone who will remind you that you are already competent and that you can meet these goals in the same way you have met many other challenges.

Tools

The following worksheet helps you to anticipate barriers and mitigate them while implementing your action plan. You can refer to Susan's completed worksheets as an example.

TABLE 7.1: BARRIERS ACTION PLANNING WORKSHEET

Category	Barrier	Impact of Barrier	How to Remove or Work Around	Support I Need to Remove or Work Around
In my thinking				
In my behavior				
In our beliefs				
In how we do things				

Susan's Worksheet

When we last met Susan, she was building her support team and defining how she wanted to communicate.

BARRIER ACTION PLANNING WORKSHEET

Category	Barrier	Impact of Barrier	How to Remove or Work Around	Support I Need to Remove or Work Around
In my thinking	Old paradigms	My reluctance to embrace new thinking may delay my desired changes	Open-minded, willing to accept the risk of change and support of my advisory team, including ongoing feedback	Internal awareness of my default approaches and external feedback
In my behavior	Tendency to follow comfortable ways	Avoidance of change will deter progress	Be open to input and advice from others regarding novel solutions and approaches	Support from upper level leadership and open-mindedness from the people I am trying to manage Feedback and reinforcement from guiding team and close colleagues
In our beliefs	Resistant to change Threat of new processes and approaches Reluctance to embrace new thinking	Continue doing the same behaviors that are preventing our advancement and that could threaten our survival in the new health care environment	Demonstrate good rationale for change Involve department leaders in the process Incentivize and reinforce new paradigms	Support from division directors when new way is questioned Leaders continually reinforce changes Provide consequences/ de-incentivize those unwilling to change

Category	Barrier	Impact of Barrier	How to Remove or Work Around	Support I Need to Remove or Work Around
In how we do things	Comfort with current approach Discomfort with building new skills	Impede our ability to capture new efficiencies	Lead by example Reward behavior changes and early adopters Provide time to adapt to and practice new skills and reinforce new thinking	Buy-in and support Integrate the new changes into overall performance management systems; rewarding new behavior and the people who quickly adopt changes

Innovative Leadership Reflection Questions

To help you develop your action plan, it is time to further clarify your direction using reflection questions. The questions for "What do I think/believe?" reflect your intentions. "What do I do?" questions reflect your actions. The question "What do we believe?" reflects the culture of your organization (i.e., work, school, community), and "How do we do this?" question reflects systems and processes for your organization. This exercise is an opportunity to practice innovative leadership by considering your vision for yourself and how it will play out in the context of your life. You will define your intentions, actions, culture, and systems in a systematic manner.

Table 7.2 contains a thorough list of questions to appeal to a broad range of readers. You will likely find some that best fit your own personal situation; focus on those that seem the most relevant. We recommend you answer one to three questions from each of the categories.

TABLE 7.2: QUESTIONS TO GUIDE THE LEADER AND ORGANIZATION

What do I think/believe?

- In what ways do I need to change my perspective or skills to succeed?
- To become more effective, what do I need to change about how I see myself, my role in health care, or the world?
- Including beliefs, what do I need to let go of to make these changes?
- What do I see as my individual role? How does this role allow me to fit in different health care organizations?
- How can I effectively grow and empower myself? How do I support my success as well as the success of the organization(s)?
- How can I benefit from my own personal growth and development?

What do I do?

- What feedback do I seek that will allow me to correct, redirect, or recalibrate my behavior and feel motivated to make necessary changes?
- How do I request clear and concise feedback that allows me to grow and supports the growth of others?
- How do I determine what I am ready to change within myself and what additional support I require for those changes I am resisting?
- What help am I willing to request? Am I investing appropriate time and/or money to support my growth? Is the commitment I am making to my personal change consistent with the results I expect to receive?
- What creative solutions can I find to increase my personal awareness? Do I track my performance against my goals using logs or reflection activities?
- How will I identify times when my behavior undermines my success?
- What will I do when I find my own behavior undermines my success?
- Can I treat my competing commitments as learning opportunities?
- How do I encourage "bad news" as well as good from my support team?
- Am I looking for opportunities to visibly demonstrate my progress as my development process unfolds?
- What am I doing to retain my support team as time goes on?
- How do I manage my transformation over the passage of time? How do I focus on living my current life while concurrently focusing sufficient time on my vision and goals?

What do we believe?

- How will my changes impact my ability to be successful, based on the organization's reward system, and given its values, goals, and culture?
- What are the stories within the organization about effective leadership? How do my personal changes position me going forward?
- What stories/narratives of the past do we need to stop telling because they no longer support our or my success?
- How can we connect prior leadership development successes to my current development effort? How can we use prior success to reinforce our ability to navigate current leadership changes?
- What parts of our past failures were attributed to leadership? Do my development changes appear positive to the organization's success, or are they threatening?
- Does our culture support the behavioral traits I am trying to develop?

How do we do this?

- What processes do we have that may serve as barriers to developing in the way I would like? Am I in a position to change the systems to remove these barriers? If so, how involved and complex will those changes be? If I cannot remove the barriers, how will I navigate around them?
- Are my changes aligned with the organization's guiding principles? If not, how do I navigate the gaps between them?
- Do the organizational structure and governance approach support my personal development? If not, what options do I have to resolve barriers to my growth?
- What early warning metrics can I use to track the impact my behavioral changes are having on others? What leading indicators will alert me before any significant issues arise?
- How can I leverage current or generally accepted leadership mastery frameworks to gain support of others and explain the changes I am trying to make?
- How do my changes fit into the current organizational reward system? If there are misalignments, what will I do to navigate the barriers and challenges?
- Have I clearly articulated the changes I want to make and asked for the support of those around me, while allowing them to maintain their success in a dynamic and changing environment?
- What communication processes do we use to provide timely feedback? How will these impact me during my development? How will my development impact others?
- What communication, if any, do I use for those who are not supporting my development or progress as a leader?
- What is the organization doing to measure, communicate, and fund the activities required for my development?

Susan's Response to Reflection Questions

We will now walk through Susan's answers to one or two questions from each section of Table 7.2. Simply follow along with Susan to answer the questions for yourself or select the questions that fit your current situation.

What do I think/believe?

- ***In what ways do I need to change my perspective or skills to succeed?***

  I have had years of experience and success in my prior role, so I know how to function well within those. I need to remember that in the new role, I need to build additional skills and let go of some prior behavioral patterns that served me well in the past but will not serve me well in the future. Years of experience can be a very valuable in dealing with daily business and personal challenges; however, the danger is in becoming too comfortable with how I have handled these challenges without considering the strategies that are appropriate to my current role.

- ***Including beliefs, what do I need to let go of to make these changes?***

I need to let go of the belief that I need to manage each individual within the department and also that I need to be fully apprised of the details of all key projects. This level of detail management served me well in the past but will cause me to fail in this role.

To let go of the details, I will need to improve my willingness and ability to hold people accountable. While I do have a belief that this change in emphasis is important, I am competitive and have a commitment and belief that I need to work harder than others. When they do not perform, I often step in to finish the task. When situations arise in which I feel that others aren't up to expectations, I need to find appropriate and kind ways to find a path forward. I need to increase emphasis on consistently setting goals and providing regular feedback without the emotional interferences regarding about my satisfaction or dissatisfaction with their goal accomplishment.

This could be a bit of a stretch for me. It is easy to determine my personal goals and aggressively move toward them. Determining the goals for a diverse group of people who are all managing a large array of projects is much more complex and will require attention.

What do I do?

- ***How do I request clear and concise feedback that allows me to grow and supports the growth of others?***

This seems like it should be an easy question—all I need to do is ask. The challenge is that I am not accustomed to asking. I have been seen as the one with the answers and now I am asking for input and feedback. I tend to struggle a bit and feel slightly uncomfortable telling others that I am working on personal leadership development. I know in my mind that this feedback is necessary and yet making the request still feels awkward.

- ***How do I encourage "bad news" as well as good from my support team?***

There is an art to receiving as well as giving feedback. It is important for me to be receptive even if the message is challenging so that I can probe for additional details in order to hear the message clearly and put the recommendations into action if they are constructive.

What do we believe?

- ***How will my changes impact my ability to be successful based on the organization's reward system, and given its values, goals, and culture?***

In the field of medicine, it is no longer about the "me;" it is always about the "we." Medicine has become an inter-professional and collaborative field. Because of the changes in the field, teamwork and developing common goals are paramount to the success.

My goal of creating a singularly focused, aligned and cohesive department emphasizes the need for teamwork. I am also building my ability to develop the team and build on their abilities to work well together.

In reviewing my goals in response to this question, it is clear to me that the culture will reward the changes I am making.

- ***What stories of the past do we need to stop telling because they no longer support our or my success?***

  I realize as a new leader in this role, I need to be sensitive to the fact that many of my prior experiences may not have relevance to the current culture of the department. I will need to learn the stories that were effective from the group's past and build on them while minimizing stories from their past that were not helpful. It will be imperative for me to show my interest in their stories and culture and build on them.

How do we do this?

- ***Do the organizational structure and the governance approach support my personal development? If not, what options do I have to remove barriers to my growth?***

  The organization provides and expects us to use onboarding, leadership development programs and coaches for department chairs when we are promoted. Thus, I believe the organization does support my personal development. They evaluate leadership success based on input from our colleagues and subordinates. This reinforces emphasis on personal growth. For many leaders, the only reason they will make development a priority is because the organization establishes it as a priority and has a low tolerance for poor-quality leaders even if they are high-quality physicians and researchers.

- ***What communication, if any, do I use for those who are not supporting my development or progress as a leader?***

  I tend to want to be positive in my attention and focus, so I will reciprocate toward those supporting me and remain as neutral and fair as possible to those who are neutral and fair to me. I realize not everyone will take an interest in my development, but I do expect them to be either supportive or remain neutral. I will not accept people undermining or blocking my success. If I learn that my team or colleagues are undermining me, I will do my best to ask for input and have constructive conversations. I will ask directly for their input and for their support.

Your Process of Taking Action

Now that you have seen the worksheets and read through Susan's narratives, it is time to complete the worksheets and answer the questions. We encourage you to complete all of the exercises and answer one to three reflection questions from each section in Table 7.2. This process serves to help you clarify what your barriers to success are, and how you will manage or remove them.

This chapter summarizes the basics for identifying barriers to your ability to successfully accomplish your goals as described in your plan. It also asks you to monitor the systems you put into place to measure your success and take corrective action. The next chapter will walk you through the process of ensuring that the changes you make are sustainable.

Resources

Books

Action Inquiry, The Secret of Timely and Transforming Leadership. Torbert and Associates.

DVD

Shadow Module 3-2-1 Process with Diane Hamilton. Integral Life Practice Series produced by Integral Institute.

What do I think/believe?

What do I do?

What do we believe?

How do we do this?

CHAPTER 8

Step 6: Embed Innovation Systematically

This is the sixth and final step in the process: Embed Innovation Systematically.

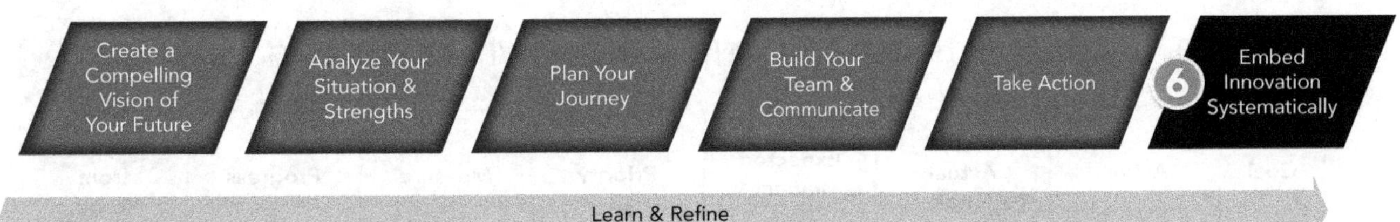

Congratulations! You have made it to the final chapter in your development process. You are now ready to shift from implementing your plan as something with a discrete end, to considering how you will integrate these changes into your lifestyle going forward. We suggest you view your leadership development as an ongoing process rather than something to check off the to-do list. Given the volume of change we now face and expect to face in the future, continual development is a must—simply to stay current. In this light, you can begin asking yourself, "What supports can I put into place to stay on track? How can I gain additional benefits from ongoing practice?"

To maintain momentum, it is critical to retain a sense of urgency and minimize any complacency that may come from early success. Be aware that it is easy to stray from your goals if you declare success based on your early results, especially when other areas of your life tug at your time and attention. One helpful shift in thinking is to see the actions you are taking as a practice. You are practicing your leadership skills in the same fashion that a professional athlete practices a particular sport. The most successful athletes are constantly working to improve, even though they may already be the best in the world. This is why many of them remain successful over a long period of time. You will need to consider a long-term commitment to activities that foster success and help maintain your momentum.

So, ask yourself, "When I see progress, what will keep me motivated to continue practicing? I need some reminder that my progress is a result of engaged practice, and my performance is likely to suffer if I do not maintain proper focus."

By this point, you may want to re-evaluate your goals and begin raising the bar. You will need to balance long-term practice that sustains progress with identifying your next developmental focus or goals.

Altogether, this step invites you to be more conscious of actions as well as tangible barriers. Identify the elements in your life that support the continual realization of your goals. Also, examine the events and relationships that interfere with your vision and goals. It is critical to remove as many barriers as possible and to stop behaviors that no longer align with your development goals.

The overall objective in this chapter is to understand your habits and choices and to confirm they are aligned with your long-term goals.

Tools

Below is a table you can use to capture and track your progress. For many people, the simple act of recording their progress in writing helps maintain their commitment. Use the following worksheet to help track your progress against each of your goals. If you would like to see a sample, review Susan's answers later in this chapter.

TABLE 8.1 PERSONAL TRANSFORMATION ACTIVITY/PRACTICE LOG TEMPLATE

Goal	Action	Record Actual Performance	Expected Impact	Priority	Measure	Progress	Feedback from Whom
Top 1	1.						
	2.						
	3.						
Top 2	4.						
	5.						
	6.						
Top 3	7.						
	8.						
	9.						

Susan's Worksheet

Susan will now walk us through her worksheets and journal entries for embedding change systematically.

PERSONAL TRANSFORMATION ACTIVITY							
Goal	**Action**	**Record Actual Performance**	**Expected Impact**	**Priority**	**Measure**	**Progress**	**Feedback From Whom**
Develop skills to effectively administer	Enhance knowledge of operating a complex department	Attended chairman leadership workshop	Clear understanding of intercon-nections within the department	1	Meet with key members of the department	Done	Department members
Build **leadership** skills and presence	Understand organizational structure of the department and intercon-nections with other elements of the organization including budgeting, HR, operations	Attended national leadership program Discuss what I learn in the program with colleagues in the department	Clear understanding of intercon-nections and reporting structures	1	Improved under-standing of organizational structure in best in class organizations compared with ours	On track	Receive certificate
	Build self-awareness and professional presence	Practice skills in meetings and presentations Journal	Improved presence and skills	2	Feedback from others	Slow	Colleagues and conference organizers
	Enhance ability to work effectively with (including manage) broad spectrum of individuals	Commit to weekly meetings with division directors	Improved team cohesion	2	Feedback from team	On track	Team
	Enhance skills in analyzing, problem-solving and decision making, and building buy-in for decisions	Attend workshop in problem solving and structured communi-cations	Improved buy-in for tough decisions	1	Track outcomes of decisions	On track	Bosses and team

PERSONAL TRANSFORMATION ACTIVITY							
Develop skills that will facilitate the team building in the department	Understand personality types and individual ability to deal with complexity and professional relationships with each employee	Assess team to determine personality types and create approaches to work across type	Retreat #2 scheduled: assessments conducted	2	Improved team dynamics	On track	Team
	Consider team-building session(s)						
	Structure departmental roles and responsibilities clearly and hold people accountable						
Functioning as "one department" focusing on meeting the mission rather than competing with one another	Address team measures and conflicting measures: align systems						
	Conduct team-building sessions to build culture that sees us as "one department" not separate and competing divisions						

Innovative Leadership Reflection Questions

To help you develop your action plan, it is time to further clarify your direction using reflection questions. Questions for "What do I think/believe?" reflect your intentions. "What do I do?" questions reflect your actions. The questions "What do we believe?" reflect the culture of your organization (i.e., work, school, community), and "How do we do this?" questions reflect systems and processes for your organization. This exercise is an opportunity to practice Innovative Leadership by considering your vision for yourself and how it will play out in the context of your life. You will define your intentions, actions, culture, and systems in a systematic manner.

Table 8.2 contains an extensive list of questions to appeal to a broad range of readers. You will likely find a few of these questions fit your own personal situation; focus on the ones that seem most relevant. We recommend you answer one to three questions from each of the categories.

TABLE 8.2: QUESTIONS TO GUIDE THE LEADER AND ORGANIZATION

What do I think/ believe?

- How do I honor the progress I have made while maintaining focus on the balance of the work that needs to be done?
- How do I deal with both profound progress and a need for continued change?
- How do I deal with unresolved issues and uncertainty as I move forward?
- How do I deal with my desire to build skills and fix issues and get back to the "real work?"
- What progress have I made as a leader/person?
- Are my assumptions still valid?
- As I have changed, am I still in the right role for my personal values and mission?
- How do I define myself as a leader? How do I think about my role and impact? How does my story about my effectiveness support or hinder my continued success?
- How does my belief about myself differ from how others see me?
- Am I still committed to the practices I developed?
- Am I willing to make these practices part of my life long-term?

What do I do?

- What do I communicate that conveys both progress and continued urgency?
- Am I visibly doing what I have committed to doing?
- Am I living up to the standards I have set for myself?
- Am I perceived as acting with integrity with regard to meeting my commitments?
- What do I do that reinforces the impact of my personal development?
- What do I do to sustain my new practices and development?
- How am I continuing to show the new behaviors I have publicly and privately committed to?
- How do I continue to sustain the practices I have started and the behavioral changes I have made?
- Have these changes become part of who I am, or will I slowly slide back to old behaviors—especially under stress or as other priorities emerge?
- Do I surround myself with others who are focused on their personal changes so that I have a reinforcement system?
- Do I continue to track and measure my progress?

What do we believe?

- What do we believe about people who are always focused on their development?
- What do we believe about ongoing development practices vs. fixing problems then moving on?
- What do we believe about how to monitor and build momentum in different areas of life?
- What do we believe about appropriate pace and focus on development and growth?
- How do our beliefs about growth impact our ability to maintain momentum?
- What recognition is appropriate from different groups in my life (colleagues, boss, family, etc.)?
- How do we see ourselves now? How has our image of ourselves changed based on my personal change?

- Will the organization's goals and values change based on my personal changes?
- How do we react to old behaviors that no longer support the organization?
- If our organizational stories about "who we are" change, do we incorporate new jargon, best practices, and human interest into emerging organizational stories?

How do we do this?

- What are the top three new behaviors others can expect to see? How will these behaviors be measured and reinforced?
- Who will remind me when I am struggling that I can make these changes?
- Do I clearly understand how my personal changes impact my work? Have I started to change the way I do my job? Have I informed others (discussed with others) how their jobs or tasks will change based on my changes? If my changes impact how we interact, have we agreed on the new way we will work together? Are we following a structured plan to perform consistently according to a new structure or guidelines?
- Do we need training to support new behaviors or interactions?
- What happens if I am not successful in meeting my top three goals? How would I like others to reinforce and/or support my behavioral changes?
- Do we have systems in place that discourage me from successfully accomplishing my top three goals?
- What processes/measures will we establish to identify behaviors that are no longer appropriate or necessary? What can I stop doing that will give me more time to practice?
- Are there any new ways to gain additional momentum to leverage existing changes and/or small wins?
- Am I reviewing measures regularly and recognizing results toward my change goals?
- Does the organization acknowledge leaders who have made the desired changes (job starts and stops) and mastered new skills? Am I being rewarded for my personal development in this system?
- Do we continue to measure and reward actions that are necessary to sustain the changes using the updated job descriptions and process metrics? Am I still a good fit within this system?
- Has the organization rewarded me with recognition, promotion, increased responsibilities, or financial rewards?
- Will others be expected to demonstrate behaviors and skills that I developed during my change? How will their changed behavior reinforce my new skills and behaviors?
- Have we sufficiently updated employee orientations and other human resources, and information technology (IT) systems to support changes in goals and values for our leaders?
- Are we reviewing objective and subjective measures regularly and recognizing desired leadership behaviors for me and others?
- Are we reinforcing actions that positively influence the larger vision while inquiring into those that do not?
- Have we developed and tracked success?

Susan's Reflection Question Responses

We will now walk through Susan's answers to one or two questions from each section of Table 8.2. Simply follow along with Susan to answer the questions for yourself, or select the questions that fit your current situation.

What do I think/believe?

- ***How do I deal with my desire to fix this issue (and accomplish my goals) and get back to the "real work?"***

  I realize I am highly results focused, and it is easier to go directly toward results. Earlier in the workbook, I talked about changes I have to make in beliefs and attitudes, and I realize that if I do not change beliefs and attitudes, I will not be able to sustain my ability to generate results. It is this knowledge that drives me to stay focused on accomplishing my goals.

- ***What progress have I made as a leader/person? Are my assumptions still valid?***

  I have made significant progress in meeting my goals. I think my assumptions about the changes required are still correct, and I am seeing the benefits to myself and my Department because of the changes I have made.

What do I do?

- ***What do I communicate that conveys both progress and continued urgency?***

  I will continue to do my best to communicate that, although short-term wins and/or gains are great, we must stay focused. Just as one good day does not make a successful month or year, we must feed off these successes and not become complacent. We need to continue to focus on progress toward long term goals and big wins.

  As a team, we recognize short-term wins and as individual I take note of my own progress and find ways to celebrate—some days this is just the simple awareness that I have met a personal milestone.

- ***What do I do to sustain my new practices and development? How am I continuing to show the new behaviors I have publicly and privately committed to?***

  I have found that leading by example is still a very strong motivator for me to continue my new behaviors and also to continue to focus on ongoing development. I am also a highly driven and self-aware person. My high standards spark my desire to want to continue to grow and create ever higher goals for myself.

What do we believe?

- ***What do we believe about appropriate pace and focus on development and growth?***

  I tend to be impatient with myself and want results too quickly. I realize my own self-imposed pace is too fast for others and also puts a lot of stress on me. With that recognition, I am trying to acknowledge that other's pace may vary and modify my level of intensity.

- ***What do we believe about ongoing development practices vs. fixing problems then moving on?***

  I believe that the ongoing developmental practice goal is to greatly reduce the need to fix problems; consequently, the goal is to be more proactive in the creation of systems, practices, and programs. Although we will never totally eliminate the need for crisis management, we will, over time, be able to reduce this to a manageable level. I believe we have made significant progress in this area, but will continue to adapt over the long term—which will have a significant positive impact on our department.

How do we do this?

- ***Are there any new ways to gain additional momentum to leverage existing changes and/or small wins?***

  One way to gain momentum is to share our successes with others. By messaging our progress and successes, we will encourage others and change their vision of our department, which can lead to gaining additional resources and motivation for continued growth. We will be seen as thought leaders, role models and productive stewards of our resources.

  We will also be seen as team player in the mission of the health system which will encourage further investment in our department.

- ***Am I reviewing measures regularly and recognizing results toward my change goals?***

  I am reviewing my goals and tracking my progress. I also receive ongoing feedback, and I track how we are proceeding to meet our department goals. I realize that my success as a leader impacts our ability to meet these goals.

  I also have regularly scheduled meetings with the medical center leadership. They provide candid feedback about our departmental progress as well as my leadership. I have developed strong relationships with these leaders, and we mutually appreciate the honest exchange of ideas.

Your Individual Process to Embed Innovation Systematically

Now that you have seen the worksheets and read through Susan's narratives, it is time to complete the worksheets and answer the questions yourself. We encourage you to complete all of the exercises and answer one to three reflection questions from each section in Table 8.2. This process serves to help you clarify what your barriers to success are and how you will manage or remove them.

In summary, this chapter helped you create an action plan and conduct thought experiments needed to sustain the changes you have invested so much time to generate. At this time in history, we culturally reinforce the idea of lifestyle changes like diet and exercise. This is also true of leadership development, awareness, and skill building. To sustain the changes you have made and continue to build on them, it is important for you to continually approach them with deliberation and a sense of presence.

In our dynamic environment, growth and development are required just to stay relevant. This is perhaps more true now than at any other time in history, where growth is now a requirement to achieve and maintain success. Leadership growth is not only a matter of conceptual and pragmatic learning, but being introspective about our relationship with ourselves and others.

Conclusion

Congratulations! If you started with the first step, you have finished the Innovative Leadership development process, and we trust you have seen a significant increase in your professional and personal effectiveness. It is time to celebrate your successes and the support you received from others! How will you acknowledge what you have accomplished? Consider reviewing your vision and SWOT analysis, and write down what you accomplished.

How will you acknowledge the support others provided? How, in your culture, do you show gratitude and appreciation? When will you celebrate with your support team, either individually or collectively? Have you already been celebrating?

What Is Next For You?

Through this workbook, we provided a framework for developing Innovative Leadership to support your success. We augmented the process with a series of reflection questions and templates that can serve as guides. Based on our work with several hundred clients, we offer this specific combination of tools and framework to create a comprehensive approach that will allow you, the leader, to define what you want to change and give you a road map to support your development.

We also provided the story of Susan to illustrate how to use the development process from a physician perspective. She uses the tools in the book and answers the questions to illustrate how a highly-effective leader would engage in development. It is through Susan's explorations that we share the practical application of this theory with you.

Now that you have completed the workbook and established a solid personal development practice, it is time to think about whether you want to enhance your practice and begin the process again. Do you want to build on what you have created and revisit parts of the workbook that may be valuable at this time? You could start from the beginning and confirm your vision and values. Future iterations will likely take less time, as you now have experience with the development process. You may find that you focus in different areas based on your growth.

Congratulations on the progress you have made on your journey toward Innovative Leadership.

Enjoy your success!

What do I think/believe?

What do I do?

What do we believe?

How do we do this?

How will you and your support team celebrate your success?

References

Boaz, Nate and Erica Ariel Fox. *Change Leader, Change Thyself*, McKinsey Quarterly 2014

Brown, Barrett. "Conscious Leadership for Sustainability: How Leaders with Late-Stage Action Logic Design and Engage in Sustainability Initiatives." Ph.D. diss., Fielding Graduate University, 2011.

Collins, Jim. *Good to Great: Why some Companies Make the Leap...and Others Don't.* New York: HarperCollins Publishers, Inc., 2001.

Cook-Greuter, Susanne. "A Detailed Description of Nine Action Logics in the Leadership Development Framework Adapted from Leadership Development Theory," www.cook-greuter.com. 2002.

Csikszentihaly, Mihaly. *Flow: The Psychology of Optimal Experience.* New York: Harper Perennial, 1990.

Fitch, Geoff, Venita Ramirez, and Terri O'Fallon. "Enacting Containers for Integral Transformative Development." Presentation: Integral Theory Conference, July 2010.

Gauthier, Alain. "Developing Generative Change Leaders Across Sectors: An Exploration of Integral Approaches," *Integral Leadership Review*, June 2008.

Goleman, Daniel. *Emotional Intelligence.* New York: Bantam Books, 1995.

Goleman, Daniel. *Working with Emotional Intelligence.* New York: Bantam Books, 1998.

Goleman, Daniel, Richard E. Boyatzis, and Annie McKee. *Primal Leadership: Learning to Lead with Emotional Intelligence.* Boston: Harvard Business School Press, 2002.

Hofstede, Geert. "Culture's Consequences: International Differences in Work-Related Values." *Sage Publications.* 1980.

Hopkins, Margaret M., Deborah A. O'Neil, Bilimoria, D. (2006). Effective leadership and successful career advancement: Perspectives from women in healthcare. *Equal Opportunities International*, 25(4), 251-271.

Hopkins, Margaret M., Deborah A. O'Neil, Kathleen FitzSimons, Philip L. Bailin, James K. Stoller (2011), Leadership and Organization Development in Health Care: Lessons from the Cleveland Clinic, in Jason A. Wolf, Heather Hanson, Mark J. Moir, Len Friedman, Grant T. Savage (ed.) *Organization Development in Healthcare: Conversations on Research and Strategies (Advances in Health Care Management, Volume 10)*Emerald Group Publishing Limited, pp.151 - 165

Howe-Murphy, Roxanne. *Deep Coaching: Using the Enneagram as a Catalyst for Profound Change.* El Granada: Enneagram Press, 2007.

Kets De Vries, Manfred. F. R., and Christine Mead. The development of the physician leader within the multinational corporation. In V. Pucik, N. M. Tichy & C. K. Barnett (Eds.), *Physicianizing management. Creating and leading the competitive organization* (pp. 187-205). New York: Wiley & Sons. 1992.

Klatt, Maryanna, Janet Buckworth, and William B. Malarkey. "Effects of Low-Dose Mindfulness-Based Stress Reduction (MBSR-ld) on Working Adults." *Health Education and Behavior* 36 (3): 601-614 (2009).

Lobel, S. A. "Physician leadership competencies: Managing to a different drumbeat." *Human Resource Management*, 29 (1): 39-47 (1990).

Maddi, Salvatore R. and Deborah M. Khoshaba. *Resilience at Work: How to Succeed No Matter What Life Throws at You.* New York: AMACOM Books, 2005.

Metcalf, Maureen. "Level 5 Leadership: Leadership that Transforms Organizations and Creates Sustainable Results." *Integral Leadership Review.* March 2008.

Metcalf, Maureen, John Forman, and Dena Paluck. "Implementing Sustainable Transformation – Theory and Application." *Integral Leadership Review.* June 2008.

Northouse, Peter G. *Leadership: Theory and Practice.* Thousand Oaks: Sage Publications, 2010.

O'Fallon, Terri, Venita Ramirez, Jesse McKay, and Kari Mays. "Collective Individualism: Experiments in Second Tier Community." Presented August, 2008 at the Integral Theory Conference.

O'Fallon, Terri. "The Collapse of the Wilber-Combs Matrix: The Interpenetration of the State and Structure Stages." Presented July, 2010 at the Integral Theory Conference (1st place winner).

O'Fallon, Terri. "Integral Leadership Development: Overview of our Leadership Development Approach." www.pacificintegral.com, 2011.

Patterson, Kerry, Joseph Grenny, Ron McMillan, and Al Switzler. *Crucial Conversations: Tools for talking when stakes are high.* New York: McGraw-Hill, 2002.

Richmer, Hilke R. "An Analysis of the Effects of Enneagram-Based Leader Development on Self-Awareness: A Case Study at a Midwest Utility Company." Ph.D. diss., Spalding University, 2011.

Riso, Don Richard, and Russ Hudson. The Wisdom of the Enneagram: *The Complete Guide to Psychological and Spiritual Growth for the Nine Personality Types.* New York: Bantam, 1999.

Riso, Don Richard and Russ Hudson. *Personality Types: Using the Enneagram for Self-Discovery.* New York: Houghton Mifflin, 1996.

Rooke, Susan and William R. Torbert. "Seven Transformations of Leadership, Leaders are made, not born, and how they develop is critical for organizational change," *Harvard Business Review*, April 2005.

Rooke, Susan and William R. Torbert. "Organizational Transformation as a Function of CEOs' Developmental Stage." *Organization Development Journal* 16 (1): 11-28 (1998).

Souba, Wiley W. *The Science of Leading Yourself: A Missing Piece in the Health Care Transformation Puzzle*, Open Journal of Leadership 2013. Vol.2, No.3, 45-55 Published Online September 2013 in SciRes (www.scirp.org/journal/ojl)

Top Issues Confronting Hospital. (2013, January 1). Retrieved from www.ache.org/pubs/research/ceoissues.cfm

Torbert, William R. and Associates. *Action Inquiry–The Secret of Timely and Transforming Leadership.* San Francisco: Berrett-Koehler Publishing, Inc. 2004.

Senge, Peter, Art Kleiner, Charlotte Roberts, Richard Ross, and Bryan Smith. *The Fifth Discipline Fieldbook: Strategies and Tools for Building a Learning Organization.* New York: Doubleday, 1994.

Terrell, Steve. Learn From Experience. *Leadership Excellence*, June 2013.

Terrell, Steve. Learning Mindset: Developing Leaders through Experience. www.trainingmag.com. March 2014.

Wigglesworth, Cindy. "Why Spiritual Intelligence Is Essential to Mature Leadership," *Integral Leadership Review*, August, 2006.

Wilber, Ken. "Introduction to Integral Theory and Practice: IOS Basic and AQAL Map." www.integralnaked.org. 2003.

Author Bio

Maureen Metcalf, MBA

Maureen is the founder and CEO of Metcalf & Associates, Inc., a management consulting and coaching firm dedicated to helping leaders, their management teams and organizations implement the innovative leadership practices necessary to thrive in a rapidly changing environment.

Maureen is an acclaimed thought leader who developed, tested, and implemented emerging models that dramatically improve leaders and organizations success in changing times. She works with leaders to develop innovative leadership capacity and with organizations to further develop innovative leadership qualities. Maureen is at the forefront of helping organizations to explore these emerging solutions for long-term organizational sustainability.

As a senior manager with two "Big Four" Management consulting firms for twelve years, Maureen managed and contributed to successful completion of a wide array of projects from strategy development and organizational design for start-up companies to large system change for well-established organizations. She has worked with a number of Fortune 100 clients delivering a wide range of significant business results such as: increased profitability, cycle time reduction, increased employee engagement and effectiveness, and improved quality.

Author Bio

James K. Stoller, MD, MS

Dr. Stoller is a pulmonary/critical care physician at the Cleveland Clinic and Chairman of the Cleveland Clinic Education Institute. He holds the Jean Wall Bennett Professorship and the Samson Global Leadership Academy Endowed Chair at the Cleveland Clinic Lerner College of Medicine. Dr. Stoller holds a Master's degree in organizational development and serves as adjunct Professor of Organizational Behavior at the Weatherhead School of Management of Case Western Reserve University. His main areas of interest are in organizational behavior regarding physician leadership development, and in pulmonary/critical care regarding COPD and alpha-1 antitrypsin deficiency.

Author Bio

Sheryl Pfeil, MD

Dr. Pfeil is an Associate Professor in the Division of Gastroenterology, Hepatology, and Nutrition, as well as the Medical Director of the Clinical Skills Education and Assessment Center at the Ohio State University College of Medicine and Wexner Medical Center. Dr. Pfeil serves on the Education and Training Committee of the American Gastroenterological Association and is a member of the Board of Directors of Alpha Omega Alpha Medical Honor Society. Her main areas of academic interest are physician leadership development and professionalism.

Author Bio

Mike Morrow-Fox, MBA

Michael Morrow-Fox, MBA, is a consultant experienced in health care, education, and non-profit management. Michael has over 20 years of experience in leading technology and human resources operations, as well as several years of full time university teaching. Michael has served as a Principle and Consultant for Metcalf and Associates, a full-time university faculty at Capital University winning a Department of Education FIPSE Grant and George Mason Program Excellence Award, as the Director of Technology Strategy for the OhioHealth Hospitals, as the Vice President of Operations for a technology start-up serving American Express, and as the Vice President of Human Resources and Talent Management for the Great Rivers Affiliate of the American Heart Association.

Michael has held Project Management Professional (PMP) Certification since 2002 and has been a Six Sigma Green Belt since 2006. His Bachelor's degree focused on Industrial Psychology and Employee Counseling and his MBA focus was on Organizational Leadership both from Franklin University; he is currently pursuing his Ed.D in Leadership from the American College of Education.

Thank you for reading!

Thank you for taking the time to read the *Innovative Leadership Workbook for Physician Leaders.*

I trust the worksheets and reflection questions you completed here will help you become a more effective leader. Because growth has a ripple effect dynamic, we welcome your suggestions, additional tools and templates. Please contact me at:

Maureen Metcalf
Metcalf & Associates, Inc.
MMetcalf@metcalf-associates.com

This is the eighth in a series of workbooks. Download other titles on Innovative Leadership at www.innovativeleadershipfieldbook.com

CPSIA information can be obtained
at www.ICGtesting.com
Printed in the USA
BVHW011053131219
566326BV00009B/345/P